Brown John

The History of the Rise and Progress of Poetry

Through It's Sic Several Species

Brown John

The History of the Rise and Progress of Poetry
Through It's Sic Several Species

ISBN/EAN: 9783337211714

Printed in Europe, USA, Canada, Australia, Japan

Cover: Foto ©Thomas Meinert / pixelio.de

More available books at **www.hansebooks.com**

THE
HISTORY

OF THE

RISE and PROGRESS

OF

POETRY,

Through it's feveral S P E C I E S.

Written by Dr. B R O W N.

—— *Fuit hæc Sapientia* quondam,
Publica privatis fecernere, facra prophanis ;
Concubitu prohibere vago ; dare jura Maritis ;
Oppida moliri ; leges incidere ligno.
Sic honor & nomen *divinis* Vatibus *atque*
Carminibus *venit.——*   HOR.

NEWCASTLE: Printed by J. WHITE and T. SAINT,
for L. DAVIS and C. REYMERS, againft *Gray's-
Inn-Gate, Holborn, London.*

MDCCLXIV.

ADVERTISEMENT.

IT is thought proper to inform the Purchafers of the " *Differtation on the* " *Rife, Union, &c. of Poetry and Mufic,*" that the Subftance of *this* Volume is contained in *That ;* which is now thrown into the prefent Form, for the Sake of fuch claffical Readers as are not particularly converfant with Mufic.

CONTENTS.

A 2   SECT.

SECT.

S E C T. X.

S E C T. XI.

S E C T. XII.

S E C T XIII.

A 3   THE

THE
HISTORY, &c.

SECTION I.

The DESIGN.

WHATEVER is founded in such *Paſſions* and *Principles* of Action, as are *common* to the whole *Race* of *Man*, will be moſt effectually inveſtigated, as to its *Origin* and *Progreſs*, by viewing Man in his *ſavage* or *uncultivated* State. Here, before Education and Art have caſt their Veil over the human Mind, its various Powers throw themſelves out, and all its Workings preſent themſelves inſtantly, and without Diſguiſe.

It may be affirmed with Truth, that, for Want of beginning our Inquiries at this early and neglected Period, and by

B   viewing

viewing Man under his State of *Civiliza-tion* only, many curious and interesting Questions have been left involved in Dark-nefs, which might have been clearly un-folded by a free and full Refearch into the Paffions, Propenfities, and Qualities of *favage* Man.

This the Writer hopes to make appear in a more *extenfive Degree*, and on Sub-jects of *higher Importance*, through the Courfe of a future Work [*a*]; of which, fome of the Principles here delivered will make an incidental Part. In the mean Time, he intends to treat the prefent Sub-ject in the Way now propofed, by dedu-cing *the Hiftory of Poetry* through its fe-veral Periods and Progreffions, from the firft great and original Fountain of *fa-vage Life* and *Manners:* This Work is not defigned as a mere *hiftorical Deduction* of *Facts;* but chiefly as an *Invefigation* of the *Caufes* that *produced* them.

[*a*] The Work advertifed at the End of this Volume.

SECT.

SECT. II.

Of Melody, Dance, and Poem, in the savage State.

BY examining savage Life, where un-taught Nature rules, we find that the *agreeable Passions* of Love, Pity, Hope, Joy, and Exultation, no less than their *Contra-ries* of Hate, Revenge, Fear, Sorrow, and Despair, oppressing the human Heart by their mighty Force, are thrown out by the three Powers of *Action, Voice*, and *ar-ticulate Sounds*. The *Brute* Creatures ex-press their Passions by the two first of These ; some by *Action*; some by *Voice*, and some by *both* united : Beyond these, *Man* has the added Power of *articulate Speech* : The same Force of *Association* and *Fancy*, which gives him *higher Degrees* and a *wider Variety* of *Passion*, gives rise to this *additional Power* of expressing those Passions which he feels.

Among the few *Savages* who are in the *lowest Scale* of the human Kind, these se-veral Modes of expressing their Passions are found altogether suited to their wretched State. Their *Gestures* are *uncouth* and *hor-*

B 2   *rid :*

rid : Their *Voice* is thrown out in *Howls* and *Roarings :* Their *Language* is like the *Gabbling of Geese.*

But if we afcend a Step or two higher in the Scale of favage Life, we fhall find this *Chaos* of *Gefture, Voice,* and *Speech,* rifing into an agreeable *Order* and *Proportion.* The natural Love of a *meafured Melody,* which *Time* and *Experience* produce, throws the *Voice* into *Mufic,* the *Gefture* into *Dance,* the *Speech* into *Verfe* or *Numbers,* as we fhall fee more at large below. The Addition of mufical *Inftruments* comes of Courfe : They are but *Imitations* of the human Voice, or of other natural Sounds, produced gradually by frequent Trial and Experiment.

Such is the Generation and natural Alliance of thefe three *Sifter-Graces, Melody, Dance,* and *Poem,* which we find moving Hand in Hand among the favage Tribes of almoft every Climate.

For the Truth of the Fact, we may appeal to moft of the Travellers who defcribe the Scenes of uncultivated Nature : All thefe agree in telling us, that *Melody, Dance,* and *poetic Song,* generally make up the ruling Paftime, adorn the Feafts, compofe compose the Religion, fix the Manners, strengthen the Policy, and even form the future Paradise, of savage Man. That having few Wants, and consequently much Leisure, the barbarous Tribes addict themselves to these alluring Arts with a wonderful Degree of Passion, unless . where their Manners are corrupted by an incidental Commerce with the Off-scum of civilized Nations. By these attractive and powerful Arts they celebrate their public Solemnities ; by these they lament their private and public Calamities, the Death of Friends, or the Loss of Warriors : By these united, they express their Joy on their Marriages, Harvests, Huntings, Victories ; praise the great Actions of their Gods and Heroes ; excite each other to War and brave Exploits, or to suffer Death and Torments with unshaken Constancy.

These are the Circumstances most *common* to the savage Tribes : Besides these, there are many *peculiar* Modes, which arise from their different Climates, Situations, Opinions, Manners. Among some Tribes the *joyous* Passions, among some the *gentle*, among others the *ferocious*, pre-

dominate

dominate and take Place. To give all the Varieties of thefe favage and feftal Solemnities, were an endlefs Labour. Let the following Account fuffice as a general Image of the reft; which is fingled out, not only becaufe it is the moft circumftantial; but likewife for the particular Relation which it will be found to bear to a following Part of this Inquiry.

The IROQUOIS, HURONS, and fome lefs confiderable Tribes, are free and independent Savages, who inhabit the northern Continent of AMERICA; and extend their Settlements from the Back of the *Britifh Colonies* to the Borders of the *Great Lakes*, along the Skirts of LOUISIANA, and down the River OHIO, towards the MISSISIPI, and the Gulph of FLORIDA. Father LAFITAU [b] gives the following Defcription of their *feftal Solemnities ;* which it is neceffary to tranfcribe at large, in order to give an adequate Idea of their Manners and Character.

" On the appointed Day, early in the " Morning, they prepare the Feaft in the " *Council-cabin,* and there they difpofe all

[b] *Mœurs des Sauvages,* tom. ii. p. 213, &c. 12mo.

" Things

" Things for the Affembly.—In the mean
" time a public Crier goes through the
" Village, and gives Notice, that the *Ket-*
" *tle* is hung on in fuch a Cabin: The
" common People, and even the Chiefs,
" bring with them their *little Kettle.* It
" doth not appear, that there is any Dif-
" tinction of Ranks among them, except
" that the *old Men* occupy the foremoft
" Matts. The Iroquoise *Women* affift
" not, that I know of, at thefe Kind of
" Feafts; nor are they invited. The *Chil-*
" *dren,* and *young Men,* who are not as
" yet chofen into the Body of Warriors,
" mount upon the Scaffolds which are
" placed over the Matts, and even upon
" the Roof of the Cabin itfelf, and look
" down through the Hole at which the
" Smoke goes out.

" While the Affembly is forming, He
" who makes the Feaft, or He in whofe
" Name it is made, *fings alone.*—The De-
" fign of this is to entertain the Company,
" on fuch Things as have Relation to the
" Subject on which they affemble. Thefe
" *Songs,* for the moft Part, are filled with
" the *Fables* of *ancient Times,* the *heroic*
" *Deeds* of their *Nation;* and are compofed
" in

" in an *antiquated Style* ; fo old, that often
" they underftand not what they fay.
" The Singer hath fome Times an Af-
" fiftant, who relieves him when he is
" fatigued : For they fing with all their
" Force.

" The Speaker then opens the Scene, by
" afking in Form, if all who are invited
" are come.   He then names the Perfon
" who makes the Feaft, he declares the
" Occafion on which it is made, and enters
" into a particular Detail of all that is in
" the Kettle. At every Thing which he
" names, the whole Choir replies by a re-
" peated Shout of Approbation.

" The Speaker then gives an Account
" of every thing, which it is of Importance
" that the Public fhould know. For thefe
" *Song-Feafts*, being made on all *weighty*
" *Occafions* which regard the *Village* or the
" *Nation ;* this is the proper Time for pub-
" lic Affairs, as that of renewing a *Name,*
" hearing *Ambaffadors*, or *proclaiming War*
" by *Song*.

" When the Orator hath done fpeaking,
" fometimes they begin to eat before they
" fing, that they may have the better Spi-
" rits : Sometimes they fing before they
" eat

" eat : If the Feaſt is to continue for the
" whole Day, the Kettle is in Part emp-
" ty'd in the Morning, and in Part re-
" ſerved for the Evening ; and in the In-
" tervals they *ſing* and *dance.*

" The Maſter of the Feaſt touches no-
" thing.   He buſies himſelf only in ſee-
" ing that the Company be ſerved, or in
" ſerving them himſelf ; naming aloud
" the Pieces which he deſtines and pre-
" ſents to each.   The beſt Morſels are
" given by Way of Preference, to thoſe
" whom he chuſeth to diſtinguiſh.

" After the Repaſt, the Maſter of the
" Feaſt, begins the *Athonront,* a *Song and*
" *Dance* peculiar to the *Men.*   They re-
" lieve each other, by beginning with
" thoſe of *moſt Conſideration,* and paſſing
" gradually down to the *Youngeſt.*   They
" have that Civility and Attention to each
" other, that every one waits till another
" of ſuperior Dignity enters the Liſts, and
" takes the Lead.

" The *Ancients* and Men of Dignity
" often do no more than *riſe* from their
" Seats ; and content themſelves, while
" they *ſing,* with making ſome *Inflexions*
" with their Head, Shoulders, and Knees,
" in

" in order to *accompany* and *fuſtain* their
" *Song*. Others ſomewhat leſs grave, take
" a few Steps, and walk along the Cabin
" around the Fires. Every one hath his
" particular *Song ;* that is, an *Air*, to
" which he *adjuſts* a very few *Words*,
" which he repeats as often as he pleaſeth.
" I have obſerved, that they even *retrench*
" or *ſtrike off* ſome *Syllables* from their
" Words, as if they were *Verſes*, or *mea-*
" *ſured* Words, but *without Rhyme*.

  " He who means to dance, begins by
" riſing from his Matt ; and the whole
" Company anſwers him by a general
" Shout of Approbation : As he paſſeth
" along before every Fire, they who ſit
" on each Side *beat* the *Meaſure* or *Cadence*
" of his *Song* by a correſpondent Motion
" of the Head ; and by throwing out con-
" tinual Shouts which they redouble at
" certain Times, where the Meaſure de-
" mands it, with ſo much Truth, that
" they never err ; and with ſuch a De-
" licacy of Ear, as the *French*, who are
" moſt practiſed in their Cuſtoms, cannot
" attain to. When he paſſeth to a ſecond
" Fire, They of the firſt take Breath :
" They of the more diſtant Fires are like-
                 " wiſe

" wife filent: But the *Time* is always *beat*
" by thofe before whofe Fire he fings and
" dances.   The Song concludes by a ge-
" neral *Ehoue!* of the whole Choir; which
" is a fecond Shout of Approbation.

" The *young* Men have their *Songs* of a
" more *lively*, and their *Dances* of a more
" *vigorous* Caft; fuch as are fuitable to
" to their Age.   When the Dance is much
" animated, they dance two or three to-
" gether, each at his own Fire : Nor does
" this Mixture ever occafion any Confufion.

" Among thefe Dances, *fome* are no more
" than a *fimple* and *noble* Manner of *march-*
" *ing* up to an *Enemy;* and of *facing Dan-*
" *ger* with *Intrepidity* and *Gaiety* of Mind.

" A fecond Sort of Dance, but ftill of
" the fame Kind, is that of the *Panto-*
" *mimes:* Which confifts in reprefenting
" an Action in the Manner in which it
" paffed, or fuch as they conceive it to
" have been.   Many of thofe who have
" lived among the Iroquois, have affured
" me, that after a Chief of War hath cir-
" cumftantially recounted, at his Return,
" all that hath paffed in the Expeditions
" he had undertaken, and the Battles he
" had fought, they who are prefent at the
" Recital

" Recital often rife on the fudden to dance,
" and reprefent thofe Actions with great
" Vivacity, as if they had been prefent:
" And all this, without any previous Con-
" cert or Preparation.

" In their *Songs* they *praife* not only
" their *Gods* and *Heroes*, but they likewife
" praife *themfelves:* In this they are not
" fparing: and are even *prodigal* in their
" *Praife* of *others*, whom they think *wor-*
" *thy* of it. He who is thus applauded,
" anfwers by a fhout of Thanks, as foon
" as he hears himfelf named.

" They are ftill quicker at *rallying* each
" other ; and fucceed to a Wonder in This.
" He who dances, takes whomfoever he
" pleafeth by the Hand, and brings him
" forth into the midft of the Affembly:
" to which he yields without Refiftance.
" Meanwhile the *Dancer* continues to *fing;*
" and fometimes in his *Song*, and fome-
" times in the *Intervals*, he throws his
" *Sarcafms* on the Patient, who hears him
" without Reply.—At every *Bon Mot*,
" loud *Peals* of *Laughter* arife along the
" *Galleries*, who *animate* this *Sport*, and
" often oblige the Patient to cover his
" Head in his Mantle.

" They

" They have another Kind of *Dance*, in
" which the whole *Choir* dances : and this
" is common both to Men and Women.
" As this is very different from the pre-
" ceding ones, they do not use it in their
" *Song-Feasts*.   Their Pretenders to *Magic*
" [c] often ordain it as an *Act* of *Religion*,
" for the *healing* of the *Sick* : it is also one
" of their Modes of *Divination*.   It is like-
" wise practised, at Times, as a mere Ex-
" ercise of *Pleasure*, at the Feasts and So-
" lemnities of the Village.   The Manner
" is as follows.   Notice is given early in
" the Morning through all the Cabins,
" for the Performance of this Ceremony :
" Every Cabin deputes a certain Number,
" either of Men or Women, who dress
" themselves in all their Finery, that they
" may go and perform their Part.   They
" all appear at the appointed Hour (which
" is proclaimed by a public Crier) either
" in the Council-cabin, or some other Place
" destined for the Purpose.   In the middle
" of the Place or Cabin they build a little
" Scaffold ; and on this they raise a small

[c] *Charlatans*,—a Word with which we have none pre-
cisely correspondent in our Language : It signifies here one
who is a Pretender to *Medicine* by the Arts of *Magic*.

" Seat

" Seat for the *Singers* who are to *accom-*
" *pany* and *animate* the *Dance.* One holds
" in his Hand a *Tambour* or little *Drum,*
" the other a *Tortoise Shell.* While thefe
" fing, and accompany their Song with
" the Sound of their Inftruments (which
" is farther Strengthened by the Specta-
" tors, who beat with little Sticks upon
" the *Kettles* that are before them) they
" who dance, go round in a circular Move-
" ment ; but without taking Hands, as
" they do in Europe. Each Dancer makes
" various Motions with his Feet and Hands,
" as he pleafeth: And though all the Move-
" ments are different, according to the
" Whim and Caprice of their Imagina-
" tion, none of them ever lofe the *Time.*
" They who are moft expert in varying
" their Poftures, and throwing themfelves
" into Action, are reckoned to excel the
" reft. The Dance is compofed of feveral
" *Returns:* Each *Return* lafts till the Dan-
" cers are out of Breath ; and after a fhort
" Interval of *Repofe*, they begin *another.*
" Nothing can be more animated than
" thefe Movements: To fee them, one
" would fay, they were a Troop of furious
" and frantic People. What muft fatigue
                                      " them

" them ftill more is, that not only by
" their Movement, but likewife with their
" Voice, they follow the Singers and their
" Inftruments to the End of each *Return;*
" which is always clofed by a general and
" loud *Oueh!* which is a Shout of Appro-
" bation, implying that the *Return* hath
" been well performed.

 " Although I have not fpoken particu-
" larly of any Nations but thofe of the
" IROQUOIS and HURONS, yet I may
" truly fay, that I have defcribed, at the
" fame Time, *all* the other barbarous Na-
" tions of AMERICA, as to what is *effen-*
" *tial* and *principal.* For though there ap-
" pears to be a great Difference between the
" *Monarchic* and *Oligarchic* State, yet the
" Genius of their favage Policy is every
" where the fame: We find the fame Turn
" for public Affairs, the fame Method of
" conducting them, the fame Ufe of fe-
" cret and folemn Affemblies, the fame
" Characters in their *Feafts*, their *Dances*,
" and their *Diverfions.*

 " The *Mufic* and *Dance* of the *Americans*
" have fomething in them extremely bar-
" barous, which at firft difgufts; and of
" which no Idea can be formed by thofe
        " who

" who have not feen and heard them. We
" grow reconciled to them by Degrees,
" and in the End partake of them with
" Pleafure. As to the Savages themfelves,
" they are fond of thefe Feafts even to
" Diftraction. They continue them whole
" Days and Nights entire; and the Shouts
" of their *Choir* are fo violent, as to make
" the Village tremble."

Thus far the learned Father LAFITAU:
For whofe Detail no Apology needs be
made to the curious Reader. But the
more particular Reafons why it is here
given at Length, will appear in the following Sections.

SECT. III.

Of the natural Confequences of a fuppofed
Civilization.

WHILE thefe free and warlike Savages continue in their prefent
unlettered State of Ignorance and Simplicity, no material Improvements in their
Song-Feafts can arife. But let us fuppofe
that the Ufe of *Letters* fhould come among
them, and, as a Caufe or Confequence of
Civilization, be cultivated with that Spirit
which

which is natural to a free and active People; and many notable Confequences would appear. Let us confider the moft probable and ftriking among thefe natural Effects.

1. Their Idea of *Mufic* in its moft *inlarged* Senfe, would probably comprehend the three united Circumftances of *Melody, Dance,* and *Poem.* For thefe three, as we have feen, being naturally conjoined, becaufe naturally producing each other, would not *feparately* command the Attention of fuch a People at their public Feftivals. Therefore *Inftrumental Melody*, without *Song*, would be little attended to, and of *no Efteem*; becaufe it would want all thofe Attractions which muft arife from the correfpondent *Dance* and *Song.*

2. In the early Periods of fuch a Commonwealth, the *Chiefs* or *Legiflators* would often be the *principal Bards, Poets,* or *Muficians.* The two Characters would commonly coalefce; for we find, that, among the favage Tribes, the *Chiefs* are they who moft fignalize themfelves by *Dance* and *Song*; and that their *Songs* rowl principally on the *great Actions* and *Events* which concern their *own Nation.*

C   3. Hence

3. Hence, their moſt ancient *Gods* would naturally be ſtyled *Singers* and *Dancers.* For the moſt ancient *Gods* of civilized Pagan Countries, are generally their early *Legiſlators*, who taught their People the firſt Arts of Life. Theſe deceaſed Legiſlators, therefore, when advanced to the Rank of Gods, would naturally be delivered down to Poſterity with the ſame Attributes and Qualities by which they had diſtinguiſhed themſelves in Life: And it appears, from the laſt Article, that theſe Qualities would naturally be thoſe of *Dance* and *Song.*

4. Meaſured Periods, or in other Words, *Rythm, Numbers,* and *Verſe,* would naturally ariſe. For meaſured Cadence, or *Time,* is an eſſential Part of Melody, into which the human Ear naturally falls. And as the ſame Force of Ear would lead the Action or Dance to correſpond with the Melody, ſo the Words or Song muſt, on a like Principle, keep Pace with *Both.* Among the *ſavage Americans* we ſee the firſt Rudiments of poetic Numbers, emerging from this Source. For " as the Means of ad-
" juſting the Words to the Air or Melody,
" they ſometimes ſtrike off Syllables from
" their

" their Words."   And fuch is the natural
Generation of *Rythm* and *Verfe*.

5. Their earlieft *Hiftories* would be written in Verfe.   For we fee, that among the
favage Tribes, the Actions of their Heroes
and Gods, and the great Events of their
Nation, make a principal Part of their
Songs.   Whenever, therefore, the Ufe of
Letters fhould come among fuch a People,
thefe *ancient Songs* would naturally be *firft
recorded*, for the Information and Ufe of
future Times.

6. Their moft ancient *Maxims, Exborta-
tions, Proverbs,* or *Laws,* would probably
be written in Verfe.   For thefe would naturally make a Part of their *Songs* of Celebration, and would by Degrees be *felected*
from thence, would in Time become the
Standard of *Right* and *Wrong*, and as fuch,
be treafured up and appealed to by the
improving Tribe.

7. Their *religious Rites* would naturally
be performed or accompany'd by *Dance*
and *poetic Song*.   For it appears from Fact
that the great Actions of their Gods and
Heroes are the moft general Subject of the
favage Dance and Song; and the common
End of Pagan Rites hath ever been, to

C 2   praife

praife the Gods of the Country, and by thefe Means (as well as by Sacrifice) to appeafe their Wrath, or fecure their Favour.

8. Their *earlieft Oracles* would probably be delivered in *Verfe*, and *fung* by the Prieft or Prieftefs of the fuppofed God. For thefe *Oracles*, being fuppofed to be *infpired* by a deceafed *Chief* (now a *Deity*) who had himfelf delivered his Exhortations in this *enthufiaftic Manner;* and being addreffed to a Tribe among whom this Mode of Inftruction univerfally prevailed, no other Vehicle but that of *Verfe* and *Song* could at firft gain thefe *Oracles* either *Credit* or *Reception.*

9. Their poetic *Songs* would be of a *legiflative* Caft; and being drawn chiefly from the Fables or Hiftory of their own Country, would contain the effential Parts of their *religious*, *moral*, and *political* Syftems. For we have feen above, that the *Celebration* of their deceafed Heroes would of Courfe grow into a *religious* Act: That the *Exhortations* and *Maxims* intermixed with thefe Celebrations, and founded on the *Example* of their *Heroe-Gods*, would naturally become the *Standard* of *Right* and *Wrong*; that is, the Foundation of

private

private Morals and *public Law:* And thus, the whole Fabric of their *Religion, Morals,* and *Polity,* would naturally arife from, and be included in their *Songs,* during their Progrefs from favage to civilized Life.

10. MUSIC, in the extended Senfe of the Word (that is, including *Melody, Dance,* and *poetic Song*) would make an effential and principal Part in the *Education* of their Children. For the important Prin- ciples of their *Religion, Morals,* and *Polity,* being delivered and inculcated in their *Songs* or *Poems,* no other Method could be devifed, which would fo ftrongly imprefs the youthful Mind with the *approved Prin- ciples* of *Life* and *Action.*

11. *Melody, Dance,* and *poetic Song,* therefore, thus *united,* muft gain a *great* and *univerfal Power* over the Minds and Actions of fuch a People. For through the Force of early and continued *Habit,* toge- ther with the irrefiftible Contagion of gene- ral *Example,* while every thing pleafing, great, and important, was conveyed through this Medium, and through this only, fuch ftrong Impreffions would ftrike themfelves into the growing Mind, as would give it its ruling Colour through

C 3   Life,

Life, and fuch as no future Incidents could
eafily weaken or efface.

12. If their warlike Charaćter continued,
the *Dance* would naturally *feparate* from
the *poetic Song*; and would itfelf become a
diftinćt Exercife or *Art*, for the Sake of increafing their Strength and Agility of Body,
as the Means of rendering them invincible
in War.   For the *Dance* or *Aćtion* of their
Song-Feafts, being only *fecondary*, and
merely an Appendage to the Song, would
not be of a Charaćter fufficiently fevere for
the fierce and ftubborn Contentions of
thofe who were deftined to the immediate
Toils of warlike Service.   .

13. After a certain Period of Civilization, the complex Charaćter of *Legiflator*
and *Bard* would *feparate*, or be feldom
united.   For as the Society grew more po-
pulous, and the increafing Arts of Life increafed the Labours and Cares of Government, the *mufical* Art (in its extended Senfe)
would of courfe be delegated by the civil
Magiftrate, to fuch Men of Genius and
Worth, as might apply it to its proper Ends,
the *Inftrućtion* and *Welfare* of Mankind.

14. In the Courfe of Time, and Progrefs
of Polity and Arts, a *Separation* of the feveral

ral *Kinds* of *poetic Song* would arife.   In the
early Periods of Civilization, the feveral
Kinds would of Courfe lie confufed, in a
Sort of undiftinguifhed Mafs, and be mingled in the fame Compofition, as Inclination, Enthufiafm, or other Incidents might
impel.   But repeated Trial and Experiment
would naturally produce a more regular
Manner; and thus, by Degrees, the feveral Kinds of Poem would affume their
legitimate Forms.

15. *Hymns* or *Odes* would be compofed,
and *Sung* by their Compofers at their feftal
Solemnities.   For thefe, in their fimple
State, are but a Kind of rapturous Exclamations of Joy, Grief, Triumph, or Exultation, in Confequence of fome great or
difaftrous Action, known, alluded to, or
expreffed: A Species of Compofition which
naturally arifeth from the favage Song-Feaft.

16. The *Epic Poem* would naturally
arife, and be fung by its Compofers at
their public Solemnities.   For it appears
above [*d*], that their earlieft Hiftories would
be written in Verfe, and make a Part of
their public Song-Feafts.   Now the *Epic
Poem* is but a Kind of *fabulous Hiftory*,

[*d*] Article 5.

C 4   rowling

rowling chiefly on the great Actions of
ancient Gods and Heroes, and artificially compofed under certain Limitations
with Refpect to its *Manner*, for the
Ends of Pleafure, Admiration, and Inftruction.

17. From an *Union* of thefe two, a certain rude Outline of *Tragedy* would naturally arife. We may fee the firft Seeds or
Principles of this Poem, in the Conduct of
the favage *Song-Feaft*. A *Chief fings* fome
great Action of a God or Heroe: The furrounding *Choir anfwer* him at Intervals,
by Shouts of Sympathy or concurrent Approbation.

18. In Procefs of Time, this barbarous
Scene would improve into a more perfect
Form: Inftead of *relating*, they would probably reprefent, by Action and Song united, thofe great or terrible Atchievements
which their Heroes had performed. For
of this, too, we find the Seeds or Principles in the favage State. " After a Chief
" of War hath recounted the Battles he had
" fought, they who are prefent will often
" rife up to dance, and reprefent thofe
" Actions with great Vivacity." If to
this we add the ufual Exclamations of the
                                    fur-

furrounding Choir, we here behold the
firft *rude Form of favage Tragedy.*

· 19. If the *Choir* fhould be *eftablifhed* by
general Ufe, and fhould animate the Solemnity by *Dance* as well as *Song*; the *Me-*
lody, Dance, and *Song* would of Courfe *re-*
gulate each other, and the *Ode* or *Song*
would fall into *Stanzas* of fome *particular*
Kind. This appears from the third Article.

20. Another Confequence of an *eftablifhed*
Choir would be an unvaried Adherence to
the *Unities* of *Place* and *Time.* For a numerous Choir, maintaining their Station
through the whole Performance, muft give
fo forcible a Conviction to the Senfes, of the '
Samenefs of *Place,* and *Shortnefs* of *Time,*
that any Deviation from this apparent
Unity muft fhock the Imagination with an
Improbability too grofs to be endured.

21. Not only the Part of the tragic *Choir,*
but the *Epifode* or *interlocutory* Part would
be alfo *fung.* For as the *Ode* and *Epic*
would be *fung* from the earlieft Periods;
fo when they became *united,* and by that
Union formed the tragic Species, they of
Courfe maintained the fame Appendage of
Melody, which Nature and Cuftom had already given them.

22. While

22. While the Nation held its *fierce* and *warlike* Character, the *tragic* Reprefentations would chiefly turn on Subjects *diftrefsful* or *terrible*. For thus they would animate each other to *Victory* and *Revenge*, by a Reprefentation of what their *Friends* had *done* and *fuffered*. Thefe Subjects would likewife be moft accommodated to the natural Tafte of the poetic Chiefs of fuch a People ; whofe Atchievements muft produce and abound with Events of Diftrefs and Terror. They alfo would be beft fuited to the Genius and Ends of their State and Polity : For as the leading View of fuch a fierce and warlike People muft be to deftroy Pity and Fear; fo this would moft effectually be done, by making themfelves familiar with diftrefsful and terrible Reprefentations. The gentle Paffions, and lefs affecting Actions, which might fill the Spectacles of a mild and peaceful Nation, would be infipid to the Tafte, and incompatible with the Character, of fuch a warlike People.

23. Their Tragedy being intended as a *vifible Reprefentation* of their ancient Gods and Heroes, it would be natural for them to invent fome Means of *ftrengthening* the *Voice*, and *aggrandifing* the *Vifage* and *Perfon*,

fon, as the Means of compleating the Refemblance : For in all Savage Countries,
the *talleft* and *ftrongeft* Men are generally
felected as their *Chiefs*.

24. As their Tragic *Poets* would be
Singers, fo they would be *Actors*, and perform fome capital Part in their own Pieces
for the Stage. For we fee thefe different
Characters are naturally united in the favage State : Therefore, till fome extraordinary Change in Manners and Principles
fhould enfue, this *Union* would of Courfe
continue.

25. *Mufical Contefts* would be admitted as
public Exercifes in fuch a State. For we
have feen, that the important Articles of
Religion, Morals, and Polity, would naturally make a Part of their public Songs :
Therefore public Contefts of this Kind
would be regarded as the beft and fureft
Means of raifing an Emulation of a moft
ufeful Nature ; and of ftrengthening the
State, by inforcing all the fundamental
Principles of Society in the moft ftriking
and effectual Manner.

26. The Profeffion of *Bard* would be
held as very honourable, and of high Efteem. For he would be vefted with a
Kind

Kind of *public Character :* and if not an
original Legiſlator, yet ſtill he would be
regarded as a *ſubordinate* and *uſeful Ser-*
vant to the *State.*

27. *Odes,* or *Hymns,* would naturally
make a Part of their *domeſtic Entertain-*
ments : and the *Chiefs* would be proud to
ſig'nalize themſelves by their Skill in *Me-*
lody and *poetic Song.* For their Songs
being the eſtabliſhed Vehicle of all the great
and important Subjects relative to the
public State ; nothing could be more ſuitable to a high Station in the Commonwealth, than a Proficiency in this ſublime and legiſlative Art.

28. When *Muſic,* that is, *Melody* and *Poem,*
thus *united,* had attained to this State of
relative Perfection, it would be regarded
as a *neceſſary Accompliſhment.* And if any
Man, or Society of Men, were unac-
quainted with its Practice and Power,
their Ignorance in this Art would be regarded as a capital Defect : For it would
imply a Deficiency in the three great
leading Articles of Education, *Religion,*
Morals, and *Polity.*

29. The Genius of their *Poem* and *Me-*
lody, would *vary* along with their *Man-*
ners :

ners: For Manners being the leading and moſt eſſential Quality of Man ; All his other Taſtes and Acquirements naturally correſpond with *Theſe;* and accommodate themſelves to his Manners, as to their chief and original Cauſe.

30. As a Change of *Manners* muſt in-fluence their *Poem* and *Melody*, ſo, by a reciprocal Action, a Change in *Theſe* muſt influence *Manners:* For we have ſeen, that They were the *eſtabliſhed Vehicle* of all the great Principles of Education.

31. A Provident Community, of Prin-ciples uncommonly ſevere, would proba-bly fix both the *Subjects* and *Movements* of *poetic Song* and *Dance*, by *Law:* This would ariſe from a Knowledge of their Influence on Manners.

32. In a Society of more libertine and relaxed Principles, the Corruption of their *Poem* and *Melody* would naturally ariſe, along with the Corruption of Man-ners, for the Reaſons now aſſigned : and the Bards, Poets, or Muſicians, would be the immediate Inſtruments of this Cor-ruption. For being educated in a corrupt State they would be apt to debaſe their Art to vile and immoral Purpoſes, as the
Means.

Means of gaining that Applauſe which would be the natural Object of their Ambition.

33. In Conſequence of this Corruption, a gradual and total *Separation* of the *Bard's* complex Character would enſue. For the *Chief* would now no longer pride himſelf on the Character of *Poet* or Performer; nor the *Man* of *Genius* and *Worth* deſcend to the Profeſſion of *Lyriſt, Singer,* or *Actor:* Becauſe theſe Profeſſions, which had formerly been the Means of inculcating every thing laudable and great, would now (when perverted to the contrary Purpoſes) be diſdained by the Wiſe and Virtuous.

S E C T. IV.

An Application of theſe Principles to the Melody, Dance, and Poem, of ancient Greece.

SUCH may ſeem to be the Conſequences which would naturally ariſe in a ſavage, free, and warlike State, ſhould *Letters* be introduced and cultivated among ſuch a ſpirited and active People. In Support of the Truth of theſe Deductions, let us now endeavour to *realize* them;

them; by fhewing that fuch Confequences
did in Faćt arife in ancient GREECE.
In the Courfe of this Review, which
will contain the Rife, Progrefs, Power,
Perfećtion, Separation, and Corruption, of
their *Melody*, *Dance*, and *Poem*, we may
perhaps be fortunate enough, on the
Principles here given, to fix fome Things
which have been held doubtful, to unfold others which have hitherto been con-
feffedly unaccountable, and to refolve
others into their proper and evident
Caufes, which have been attributed to
fuch Caufes as never had Exiftence.

1. " Their Idea of *Mufic*, in its moft
" inlarged Senfe, comprehended the three
" united Circumftances of *Melody*, *Dance*,
" and *Poem*."—This appears from the
concurrent Teftimony of many ancient
Authors: The following one from the
Alcibiades of PLATO may alone be a fufficient Authority. " *Socr.* Tell me firft,
" what Art is that, to which it belongs
" properly to *fing*, to *play*, and *dance*?
" Cannot you find a Name for this com-
" prehenfive Art?—*Alcib.* I cannot.—*Socr.*
" Try a little: Who are the Goddeffes that
" prefide over this Art?—*Alcib.* Do you
                                    " mean

" mean the MUSES?—*Socr.* I do: Confi-
" der then what Name the Art receives
" from them.—*Alcib.* You feem to hint
" at MUSIC.—*Socr.* You are right [*e*]."—
The fame Truth is no lefs evident from
the circumftantial Account which ATHE-
NÆUS gives of the old ARCADIAN *Mufic;*
which, in its general Acceptation, included *Melody, Dance,* and *Song* [*f*]. It
appears, then, that this Combination or
Union of thefe three *Sifter-Graces* arofe naturally in ancient GREECE, from an Improvement of the *favage* State into a cer
tain Degree of *Civilization.* They needed
no *Art* to joyn them: For as they *naturally* produce each other, and are naturally conjoyned in the favage and uncultivated State, this Union would of Courfe
continue, till fome violent Change in Manners or Principles fhould break that Union
which Nature had eftablifhed.

2. " In the earlieft Periods of the
" *Greek* States, their Legiflators were often
" Bards, or their Bards were Legiflators."
Such, in a more eminent Degree, were
APOLLO, ORPHEUS, AMPHION, LINUS,

[*e*] PLATO, ALCIBIADES.   [*f*] *Deipnofoph,* l. xiv.

and

and MUSÆUS [g]. Of this Rank too, was
THALES the *Cretan* Lawgiver; who compofed Laws in Verfe, and fung them
to his Lyre [h]. It hath been generally
fuppofed, that the ftory'd Power of their
Lyres and Songs meant no more, than
by a metaphorical Expreffion to convey
a ftrong Idea of their Eloquence and legiflative Art, in producing *Order* from
Confufion. Thus PLUTARCH tells us, that
" the Ancients reprefented the Statues of the
" Gods with Mufical Inftruments in their
" Hands, not as being really Lyres or
" Flutes ; but becaufe they thought, that
" nothing fo much fuited the Character
" and Office of the Gods, as *Harmony* and
" *Order* [i]." Thus too, a noble Writer
of our own Country declares his Opinion,
and fays, that " *Tradition,* which foon
" grew *fabulous,* could not better reprefent
" the firft *Founders* or Eftablifhers of large
" Societies, than as *real Songfters* [k]." But
real Songfters, beyond Doubt, they were;
nor was Tradition *fabulous* in thus reprefenting them. For from a View of human

[g] PLATO *de Rep.* l. ii.   [h] STRABO *Geog.* l. x.
[i] PLUT. *de Procreat. Anima,* &c.
[k] *Characterifics,* vol. i. p. 237.

D   Nature

Nature as emerging from the favage State,
it is evident, that the *Song* and *Lyre* (as
foon as the Lyre was invented) muft be
the natural Means or Inftruments of Civilization, by conveying the Legiflator's Precepts to the furrounding People: Becaufe
we have feen that, among the favage
Tribes, the *Chiefs* are proud to fignalize
themfelves by *Song ;* that they *prefide* at
the *Song-Feafts;* and that their Songs rowl
principally on the great Actions, Affairs,
and Events of their own Nation.—A
concurrent Proof of this natural Union of the Bard's and Legiflator's Office might be drawn, were it neceffary,
from the Name which the old THESSA-
LIANS gave their *Magiftrates:* They ftyled
them τροοχκηρις or " the Leaders of the
" Dance and Song-Feaft [*l*] :" A Circumftance which plainly points out its
own Origin.

3. " Their moft ancient Gods were
" ftyled *Singers* and *Dancers.*" Thus Ho-
RACE calls APOLLO the *Singer* [*m*]. PIN-
DAR ftyles him the *Dancer* [*n*]. HOMER,
or the Author of the Hymns that pafs

[*l*] LUCIAN. *de Saltatione.* [*m*] *Ep. ad Pifones.* [*n*] *Ode.*

under

under his Name, gives him the fame Appellation [o]. Rhea, the Mother of Jupiter, is faid to have taught her Priefts the Art of *Dancing*, both in Phrygia and Crete [p]: As Castor and Pollux inftructed the *Lacedemonians* in the fame Art [q]. Eumelus or Arctinus the *Corinthian* brings in even Jupiter himfelf *dancing*, in thefe Words,

Among them danc'd the Sire of Gods and
Men [r].

Whence it arofe, that thefe ancient Gods were reprefented as *Singers* and *Dancers*, and vefted with a Quality which at firft Sight feems altogether foreign to their Character, hath not as yet been accounted for. We now fee the true and natural Origin of thefe Appellations. For the moft ancient Gods, among the civilized *Greeks*, were their early Legiflators, who taught the favage Tribes the firft Arts of Life. Thefe deceafed Legiflators, therefore, when advanced to the Rank of Gods, were naturally delivered down to Pofterity, with the fame Attributes or

[o] *Hymn. in Apollinem.*   [p] Lucian. *de Saltatione.*
[q] Ibid.   [r] *Apud* Athenæum *Deipn.* l. i.

D 2   Qua-

Qualities by which they diftinguifhed themfelves in Life : and it appears from a View of the *Chiefs* of the favage Tribes, that thcfe Qualities would naturally be thofe of *Dance* and *Song*.

4. " Meafured Periods, or, in other " Words, Rythm, Numbers, and Verfe, " did naturally arife." The general Reafon is affigned in the fourth Article of the laft Section ; and needs not to be repeated here. But as fome particular Confequences arife from this Foundation, relative to the moft ancient *Hiftory*, *Laws*, and *Oracles*, thefe will deferve a feparate Confideration.

5. " Their earlieft Hiftories were writ- " ten in Verfe." This Fact is indifputable ; but feems not, as yet, to have been refolved into its true Caufe. STRABO informs us, that, " The Poetic Form firft appeared : " They who imitated it, dropped the Mea- " fure : Such were CADMUS the *Milefian*, " PHERECYDES and HECATÆUS [*s*]". Thefe were the firft *Greek* Hiftorians who writ in Profe. Another learned Ancient confirms this Account ; and fays,

[*s*] STRABO, l. i.

" In

" In thefe early Times, fo general was
" the Inclination to Rythm and Numbers,
" that all Inftruction was given in Verfe:
" There was neither *Hiftory* nor *Philofophy*,
" nor any Action to be defcribed, but
" what was dreffed by the *Mufes* [*t*]."
Not only the *Greek* Writers give a concurrent Teftimony concerning the Priority
of *hiftorical Verfe* to *Profe*, but the Records of all Nations unite in confirming
it. The oldeft Compofitions among the
Arabs are in Rythm or rude Verfe;
and are often cited as Proofs of the Truth
of their fubfequent Hiftory [*u*]. The Accounts we have of the *Peruvian* Story
confirm the fame Fact: For Garcilasso
tells us, that he compiled a Part of his
Commentaries from the *ancient Songs* of the
Country [*w*]. Nay all the *American* Tribes
who have any Compofitions, are found
to eftablifh the fame Truth [*x*]. Northern Europe contributes its Share of
Teftimony: For there, too, we find the
Scythian or *Runic* Songs (many of them
hiftorical) to be the oldeft Compofitions

[*t*] Plutarch.　[*u*] *Hift. de las Guerras Civil. de
Grenada.*　[*w*] *Comment. Real.* [*x*] Lafitau.

　among

among thefe barbarous Nations [*y*]. ODIN is faid to have boafted, that " his Runic " Poems were given him by the Gods [*z*]." A Circumftance which proves them to have been of the higheft Antiquity.

The Fact, then, is clear and certain: And as it is fomewhat myfterious to common Apprehenfion, various Solutions have been attempted by the Learned; though, in my Opinion, without Succefs. I fhall give them, as they appear in various Writers.

LONGINUS hath aimed at fomething like a Reafon, in the following Paffage; " Meafure belongs *naturally* to Poetry, as " its Province is the Defcription and *Lan-* " *guage* of the *Paffions*; together with *Fic-* " *tion* or Fable, which *produce Numbers.* " Hence it was that the Ancients (even in " their common Difcourfe) ufed Meafure " and Verfe, rather than Profe [*a*]." It can hardly be neceffary to obferve, that the celebrated Critic, in this Paffage, gives a mere *Affirmation* inftead of an *Argument.*

[*y*] BARTHOLIN. *de Contemptu Mortis*, &c. HICKES *Thef. Septentr.* [*z*] SHERINGHAM *Orig. Gent. Angl.* [*a*] LONGIN. *de Metr.*

He

He fays, indeed, " that the Language of the
" Paffions, and Fiction, naturally produce
" Meafure and Numbers :" But the Reafon
is ftill to feek. It were to be wifhed, that
in many Parts of his Writings, he had
not given us more Inftances of his fine
Tafte, than his Power of Reafoning.

A learned Modern of our own Nation
hath try'd his Talent in this curious
Queftion. " They (the Ancients) thought,
" it would feem, that Language was the
" firft Tamer of Men; and took its Ori-
" gin to have been certain rude accidental
" Sounds, which that naked Company of
" fcrambling Mortals emitted by Chance.
" Upon this Suppofition it will follow,
" that at firft they uttered thefe Sounds in
" a *much higher Note* than we do our
" Words now ; occafioned, *perhaps*, by
" their falling on them under fome Paf-
" fion, Fear, Wonder, or Pain ; and then
" ufing the fame Sound, either when the
" Object or Accident recurred, or when
" they wanted to defcribe it by what they
" felt from its Prefence. *Neither* the *Syl-*
" *lables* nor the *Tone* could be *afcertained :*
" but when prompted by the Return of
" the Paffion, under which they invented

" them

" them, they *extended* their *Throats* and
" put feveral of thefe Marks together,
" they would *feem* to *fing*. Hence ανδαιη
" fignified at firft fimply to *fpeak*, or utter
" the Voice; which now, with a fmall
" Abbreviation (αδω) fignifies to *fing:*
" And hence came the ancient Opinion,
" which appears fo *ftrange* to *Us*, that
" Poetry was before Profe [*b*]." Here we
fee an ingenious Writer toiling in vain
to prop a miftaken Principle. For, to
omit all the weak Parts of the Paragraph
which might expofe it to Ridicule, if neither *Syllables* nor *Tones* could be *afcertained*,
it follows, that neither *Meafure* nor *Melody*
could arife; and therefore it muft even
continue to appear as ftrange as ever,
" that Poetry fhould be before Profe."

Mr. DE VOLTAIRE talks more fpeci-
oufly (after ARISTOTLE and PLUTARCH
[*c*]) on this Subject. " Before HERODO-
" TUS, even Hiftory was not written but
" in Verfe among the GREEKS, who had
" borrowed this Cuftom from the ancient
" EGYPTIANS, the wifeft, the beft policed,

[*b*] *Enq. into the Life* of HOMER, p. 38.
[*c*] See the following Articles.

" and

" and the moſt knowing People upon
" Earth. This Cuſtom was very *reaſona-*
" *ble :* for the End of Hiſtory was to pre-
" ſerve to Poſterity the *Memory* of thoſe
" few great Men, whoſe Example might be
" of Service to Mankind. They only writ
" what was worthy of being retained by
" Heart. This is the Reaſon why they
" laid hold of the Harmony of *Verſe ;*
" that they might aid the *Memory.* And
" hence it was, that the firſt *Philoſo-*
" *phers, Legiſlators,* and *Hiſtorians,* were
" all *Poets* [d]."

As this is the moſt plauſible Reaſon
that hath ever been aſſigned for this
myſterious Fact, it will deſerve a particular Conſideration. The Cauſe aſſigned
ſeems, therefore, to reſt on no probable
Foundation, for the following Reaſons.

Firſt, becauſe it ſeems to take for granted the Exiſtence of the very Thing which
it is ſaid to have produced. If we ſup-
poſe Rythm, Numbers, and Verſe, to exiſt
and be in general Uſe, they would undoubtedly become the natural Means of
Memory and Record among a barbarous

[d] *Preface à Oedip.*

People.

People.   But to *invent* the Vehicle of
Rythm, from a *Forefight* of its being the
beft Inftrument of Memory, without any
prior Impulfe from unaffifted Nature,
feems altogether incompatible with the general Character of the favage Tribes: For
in the Period of favage Manners, the
Power of *abftract Reafoning* is always *weak*,
and is often found to have *no Place.*

Again : The *Univerfality* of the Fact
adds greatly to the Improbability of the
Caufe affigned. Though we fhould fuppofe it poffible or probable, that one favage Chief might by Dint of Reafon
ftrike out this new Method of recording
Hiftory ; yet that *All* favage Chiefs, in
every known Age and Climate, fhould
unite in the *fame* Contrivance, is highly
improbable. If one of more exalted Capacity delivered his Stories in Verfe,
another of inferior Reach and Invention
would naturally give them to Pofterity
in plain Profe: Nay, the acknowledged
Difficulty of *Verfification* would naturally
make the *profaic* Manner the more *com-*
mon, though lefs effectual Method of the
two.   Now, the contrary to this is acknowledged to be true, even by thofe
who

who contend for the Truth and Sufficiency of the Caufe affigned. The *Univerfality* of the Fact is allowed by All. Such an univerfal Coincidence, therefore, muft fpring from fome other Caufe, fuch as arifeth unalterably from Nature, and takes Place among the favage Tribes in an univerfal and unvaried Manner.

Farther: If the ancient Songs, prior to Profe in every Nation, had been *coolly compofed* for the Sake of *Tradition* and *Information only*, they would have been *circumftantial* and *precife*: Whereas the contrary appears in their Conftruction: They are generally *vague* and *enthufiaftic*; and bear all the Marks of being the genuine Effects of favage *Paffion* and *Enthufiafm*. So far are they from containing any regular *Series* of Facts, that Facts are often *hinted* only; while the mere *Celebration* of the Heroe forms the chief Weight and *Burthen* of the *Song*.

Laftly, the univerfal Connection of the *old Poetry* with *Melody*, and the unvary'd Cuftom of *finging it*, amounts to the ftrongeft Proof, that the mere End of *Memory* and *Tradition* could not be its original Caufe. For had the fole Intention

tion of the Song been that of *Record only*,
a *mere Recitation* of the Verfes would
have anfwered the fame Purpofe. And
we may affirm it to be a *moral Impoffibi-
lity* that an univerfal Union of Verfe and
Melody could have taken Place on this
Foundation.

Since, therefore, the Caufe hitherto affigned feems altogether inadequate to the
Effect; can we reafonably entertain a
Doubt, in refolving it into that Principle which we have already found univerfally predominant in favage Life? I
mean, the natural Paffion for *Melody* and
Dance, which neceffarily throws the accompanying *Song* into a *correfpondent
Rythm*. Hence, the Ufe of Rythm and
Verfe muft naturally arife in GREECE
(as in every other Country emerging from
Barbarity) becaufe Melody, Dance, and
poetic Song, made a principal Employment
of their favage State. And hence, their earlieft Hiftories muft of courfe be written
in Verfe; becaufe the Actions of their
Gods and Heroes made a principal Part
of their Songs; and therefore, when the
Ufe of Letters came among them, thefe
ancient Songs were naturally *firft* recorded,

ed, that is, they became their earlieſt *Hiſ-tories*, for the Information and Uſe of future Times.

As this Cauſe, when viewed in itſelf, ſeems amply and clearly to account for the Effect, ſo it will receive farther Confirmation, if we conſider how naturally it removes all thoſe Objections which load the Opinion here controverted. For it neither requires nor ſuppoſeth any Power of *abſtract Reaſoning* among the *ſavage* Tribes, but is the mere Effect of *Paſſion* and uncultivated Nature. Its Univerſality, therefore, becomes highly probable; becauſe the Principles of ſavage Nature (making Allowance for the Difference of Soil and Climate) are every where the ſame. The *Genius* of the ancient Songs of every Nation adds new Degrees of Evidence: For they are generally irregular and enthuſiaſtic; and therefore the genuine Productions of *unlettered Enthuſiaſm.* Laſtly, their univerſal Connexion with *Melody*, and the unvary'd Practice of *ſinging* them, comes up to a full and direct Proof, of the Reality of the Cauſe now aſſigned.

It muſt not be diſguiſed, that the moſt learned VOSSIUS was ſo ſtruck with the

Dif-

Difficulty of accounting for this Appearance, that he thinks it beſt to deny the Fact.
" To me the contrary ſeems true ; that
" Proſe was firſt written, and then Poetry.
" 'Tis natural to walk on Foot before we
" mount on Horſeback ; and it is certain
" that Men firſt *ſpoke* in *Proſe* and *then*
" in *Numbers.*   We have nothing more
" ancient than the Writings of Moses ;
" and theſe are in Proſe, with Songs in-
" termixed [*e*]."   On this Reaſoning it
may be remarked, that although it be
certain that Men *ſpoke* in *Proſe* before
they *ſpoke* in *Verſe ;* yet the Conſequence
follows not, that therefore they muſt
write in *Proſe* before they *writ* in *Verſe.*
The ſole Queſtion is, what would be
deemed beſt worth recording, on the firſt
Riſe of the *writing Art?*   Surely, the Actions and Celebrations of their Anceſtors,
Gods, and Heroes ; Now theſe, we have
already ſeen, muſt naturally make the
chief Subject of their feſtal Songs ; and
therefore their *feſtal Songs* were of Courſe
the *firſt* Things *written* or *recorded.*

[*e*] *De Artis Poët. Nat. et Conſt.* c. i.

With

With refpect to the Inftance alledged by the learned Critic, of the Writings of MOSES, and the Practice of ancient EGYPT, this, when properly explained, will confirm the Truth of the Caufe here given. MOSES, we know, was learned in all the Wifdom of the *Egyptians*: EGYPT was in his Time become a *polifhed Nation*: and therefore, according to the natural Courfe of Things (as will appear below) *Profe* had been introduced before the Time of MOSES, as it was afterwards in GREECE by HECATÆUS and others. As to the intermixed Songs in the Writings of MOSES, it is now a Point agreed among the Learned, that they are written in *Meafure*; and correfpond in all Refpects with the Principle here delivered. And that *Poem* was the oldeft Form of Compofition in EGYPT, we learn clearly from two ancient Writers: The Firft informs us, that their Mufic and Songs had continued unchanged, for upwards of three thoufand Years [*f*]: The other gives a more particular Account of their Nature, and Manner of being fung. " The

[*f*] PLATO *de Rep.* l. vii.

" firft

" firft of the Priefts who ufed to appear in
" the religious Proceffion, was a *Chora-*
" *gus, Bard,* or *Singer,* who carried the
" Symbol of Mufic, and could repeat by
" Heart the two firft Books of MERCURY;
" the firft containing *Hymns* in Honour
" of the Gods ; the fecond containing
" *Sentences* or *Maxims* for the Conduct of
" a King [*g*]."

6. " Their moft ancient *Maxims, Ex-*
" *hortations, Proverbs,* or *Laws* were
" written in *Verfe.*" Having traced the
Antiquity of *Song* and *poetic Hiftory* to
its true and natural Caufe, the prefent Article will be of eafy Difcuffion. For as
the Greek Songs and poetic Stories were
fraught with the great Actions of their
Gods and Heroes, fo *Maxims* of *Exhor-*
tation, which in barbarous Countries hold
the Place of *Laws,* muft of Courfe make
a Part of thefe public Songs, muft by
Degrees be felected from them, and in
Time be appealed to, as the *Standard* of
Right and *Wrong.*

However, as ARISTOTLE hath hinted
at another Caufe, the flighteft Conjecture

[*g*] CLEMENS ALEXANDR. *Stromat.* l. vi.

of

of fo great a Name muft not pafs unnoticed.   He puts the Queftion thus.
" Why are many *Songs* called by the
" Name of *Laws?* Was it becaufe, before
" the Invention of the Art of Writing,
" *Laws* were *fung*, left they fhould be *for-*
" *gotten* [*h*]?" On this Paffage it will be
only neceffary to remark, Firft, that the
Opinion is delivered as a mere Conjecture.
Secondly, that all the Difficulties which
load the common Opinion concerning the
firft Rife of *poetic Hiftory*, lie equally heavy
upon *this:* And laftly, that the fame Solution leads us up to the true Caufe, on the
natural Principles of the *favage Song-Feaft.*
This Solution may, perhaps, in the Opinion of fome, receive additional Confirmation from the concurrent Authority of
CASAUBON; who declares it his Belief
(though he affigns no Reafon) that the
Songs called *Nomoi* were *Fragments* of ancient Poetry, which had been felected and
preferved on Account of their Utility [*i*].

[*h*] *Problem.* Sect. xix. Art. 28.   He is followed in
this Opinion by the learned Mr. GOGUET, in his late
Book on Laws and Government.   " The earlieft Legi-
" flators fet their Laws to Mufic, that they might be
" more eafily retained." *Tom.* ii. *L.* i. *Art.* 8.
   [*i*] *In* LAERT.

                    E   7. " Their

7. " Their earlieft *religious Rites* were
" performed or accompanied by *Dance* and
" *poetic Song.*" The *Orgies* of BACCHUS,
celebrated in this Manner, were famed
through all the Ages of Antiquity.
STRABO tells us, that " the *Greeks* RE-
" TAINED the Cuftom *common* to the *Bar-*
" *barians,* of celebrating their Sacrifices to
" the Gods with Mufic, confifting of Dance,
" Melody, and poetic Song:" And highly
extols this Practice, " as tending to unite
" the Soul with God [k]." PLUTARCH
adds his Teftimony, and informs us, that
in GREECE " the firft Application of Mufic
" was to religious Ceremonies, in Honour
" of the Gods [l]." All this flows naturally
from the View we have given of favage
Life and Manners: For we have feen that
the Praifes of their Chiefs are the moft general Topic of the favage Dance and Song;
and the *Grecian Gods* were no other than
their *deceafed Chieftains.*

8. " Their earlieft *Oracles* were delivered
" in Verfe, and fung by the Prieft or Prieft-
" efs of the fuppofed God." The natural
Caufe of this Fact hath been affigned in

[k] STRABO, l.   [l] PLUT. *de Mufica.*

the

the Article which correfponds with this. The Ancients knew and confeffed the Fact, but were fo entirely ignorant of the true Caufe, that they *laboured* more in this Point, than even in accounting for the Rife of *poetic Hiftory* and *Laws*. This will appear from PLUTARCH, who hath written a Difcourfe on the following Queftion, " Why the PYTHIA no longer gives " her Oracles in Verfe?" Now, before he affigned the Caufes why this Practice of *Oracular Verfe* had *ceafed*, it was natural that he fhould enquire how it firft *began:* And the Caufes (if fuch they may be called) which he affigns, are thefe.

Firft, " The ancient Times produced a " Race of Men, who had naturally, and " from *bodily Temperament*, a ftronger Turn " for Poetry." Secondly, " There was a " Time, when, inftead of the Art of Wri- " ting, Men ufed Metre, Verfe, or Songs ; " adapting Hiftory, and other the weigh- " tieft Subjects, to Poetry and Mufic." " Thus they celebrated the Gods ; and " told their Fables in Verfe, fome through " the Force of *Genius*, and others by the " Power of *Cuftom*." " Therefore the God " permitted the Application of Verfe and

E 2   " Song

" Song to his Oracles, and would not
" drive the Mufes from his Tripod."
Thirdly, " The Utility of Poetry is in
" nothing more confpicuous, than in its
" Affiftance to the *Memory*, by the Means
" of Numbers. The Ancients had great
" Need of This, beyond the Moderns, be-
" caufe the Oracles referred to Perfons,
" Things, and Places, which were often
" unknown to them [m]."

Thus the learned PLUTARCH; whofe
weak Reafonings (becaufe he wanted Facts
to lead him to the Truth) hardly need
a Confutation. For how came it fo to
pafs, that the firft Race of Men were by
natural bodily Temperament of a *ftronger
Turn* to *Poetry?* How came it fo to pafs,
that they told their Fables in Verfe, fome
by the Force of *Genius*, others by the
Power of *Cuftom?* Thefe Affirmations take
for granted the very Point in Queftion.

With Refpect to the laft Reafon which
the great Author affigns, " The Utility of
" Numbers, as an Affiftance to the Memo-
" ry;" This, when applied to *Oracles*, is

[m] PLUT. *Diff. Cur nunc Pythia non reddat ora-
cula carmine.*

not

not only incumbered with all the Difficulties which load the common Syftem
concerning the Origin of *poetic Hiftory*
and *Laws* ; but is contrary to the clear
Evidence of Facts, which affure us that
the poetic Oracles of DELPHI were the
Effect of *Enthufiafm.* DIODORUS gives a
particular Account of the Rife and Eftablifhment of this Oracle, from the fole
Principle of *Enthufiafm* [m]. And PAU-
SANIAS informs us, that HEROPHILE
was a very ancient Prieftefs ; and that
" fhe delivered her prophetic Infpirations
" with frantic Geftures, and in heroic
" *Verfe* and *Song* [n]." PLUTARCH tells
us farther concerning this *favage Heroine*,
that " fhe is faid to have *celebrated Her-*
" *felf* in her *Songs ;* and boafted, that fhe
" fhould not ceafe to prophecy after her
" Death : That fhe would afcend to the
" Moon, and be metamorphofed into that
" Face which we fee in the Moon's Body
" [o]." Thefe Paffages compared with
what hath here been delivered on the
favage Song-Feafts, unveil the true Origin
of the old *poetic Oracles* of GREECE.

[m] L. xvi.   [n] PAUS, *in Phocicis.*   [o] *Loco fupra
citato.*

E 3   And

And the whole Account of the *Self-Cele-*
brations of HEROPHILE, her frantic *Gef-*
tures, *Verfe,* and *Song,* contains a true
Picture of an *enthufiaftic Savage :* For it
appears above, " that Mufic, Dance, and
" Song, are one of the common Modes
" of *Divination* among the favage IRO-
" QUOIS [*p*]."

9. Their *poetic Songs* were of a *legifla-*
tive Caft; and being " drawn chiefly from
" the Fables or Hiftory of their own
" Country, contained the effential Parts of
" their *religious, political,* and *moral* Syf-
" tems." We have feen above that the Celebration of their deceafed Heroes became
naturally a *religious Act :* That the *Maxims*
or *Exhortations* intermixed with thefe, and
founded on the *Example* of their Heroe-
Gods, became of Courfe the *Standard* of
Right and *Wrong,* that is, the Foundation
of *private Morals* and of *public Law :*
Having no *Revelation* from Heaven, thefe
Songs naturally became their *religious, po-*
litical, and *moral* CODE : and thus the
whole Fabric of their *Religion, Morals,* and
Polity, arofe from their *Song-Feafts,* in their
Progrefs from *favage* to *civilized* Life.

[*p*] See the Paffage from LAFITAU.

The

The Records that remain concerning the *Bards* of ancient GREECE unite in confirming this Principle. Of this illuftrious Catalogue, LINUS was perhaps the firft : He writ the Exploits of the firft BACCHUS ; and fung the Generation of the World and the Rife of Things [*q*]. PAMPHO is fuppofed to have been his Difciple : And He compofed *Hymns* in Honour of the Gods ; and fung the Rape of PROSERPINE by PLUTO [*r*].

The next great poetic and mufical Sage was ORPHEUS: He is faid to have fung of *Chaos* and *Creation ;* and a Variety of other Subjects *religious* and *philofophical* [*s*]. Some fine Fragments remain under his Name ; but there is Reafon, from fome internal Marks in the Compofition, to believe them fpurious.

MUSÆUS is faid to have been the Difciple of ORPHEUS : He, too, writ *Hymns* and *Prophecies*, and fung the Motions of the *Stars*, and the Battles of the *Giants* [*t*]. THAMYRIS was not lefs diftinguifhed by

[*q*] DIODORUS, l. iii. and LAERTIUS.
[*r*] PAUSANIAS *in Bœoticis*   [*s*] SUIDAS *in Orpheo.*
[*t*] LAERTIUS *in Proæm.*

E 4   the

the *legiſlative* Genius of his Songs: For he was not only the Author of a *Titan's War;* but celebrated the Gods in *Hymns,* and ſung the *Generation* of the *World* [*u*].

Theſe are the moſt celebrated *Bards* of ancient GREECE, whoſe Songs have periſhed in the Wreck of Time. If we come down to the moſt famous of thoſe, whoſe Writings have been preſerved, we ſhall find their Songs compoſed in the ſame *legiſlative* Style and Genius.

HESIOD ſeems to ſtand at the Head of theſe, in the Order of Time. And his *Theogony* is a living Witneſs how far HIS *legiſlative* Turn accords to the Principles here delivered. He gives, in Form, the *Generation* of all the *Gods* of GREECE; and mixeth his Narration with their *Acts* and *Praiſes.*

HOMER appears next in the Order of Time: And in his unrivaled Songs we find the *Religion, Polities,* and *Manners* of ancient GREECE diſplayed with all the Appearances of Truth, becauſe delivered with all their *Imperfections.* During the early Periods of Civilization, the *legiſlative*

[*u*] SUIDAS *in Tham.*

Art

Art is always of an *imperfect* Form. In the rude Progrefs of barbarous Manners, the *moral* Ideas are *confined*, and little diftinguifhed. If the People be fierce and warlike (as were the Tribes of GREECE) Strength, Courage, Agility, and Cunning, are the ruling Virtues. Hence it follows, that the Pictures both of *Gods* and *Men* will accord to this Principle in fuch a Period: And hence many of the Fables of HOMER himfelf were of a Caft fo different from the Spirit of *improved Legiflation*, that PLATO refufed them Admittance into his Republic [*w*].

And here, while we acknowledge HOMER as the fupreme Painter of natural Manners, and of a Genius truly *legiflative* according to the Principles of his Time;

[*w*] *De Rep.* l. ii, iii.—It is generally affirmed and believed, that PLATO was for banifhing Poetry, without Exception, from his perfect Republic. So far is this from being true, that he affirms directly, " that he " only means to banifh That which is pernicious; but " to retain That which is ufeful." [*De Rep.* l. x.] Nay, he hath written a whole Book [*De Leg.* l. ii.] to prove the Utility of *Mufic* in the Education of Youth: through the Courfe of which, it is evident, that in His Idea, *Poetry* makes the moft effential Part of *Mufic*.

critical

critical Juſtice demands, that we take off
ſome of thoſe falſe Colourings of Praiſe,
which both Ancients and Moderns have
laviſhed on him, in Regard to the Excellence of the *Morals* which he taught.
HORACE, it is well known, hath ſet him
above the old Philoſophers, as a Teacher
of all Virtue [x]. PLUTARCH in his Life
of HOMER, hath advanced the ſame Po-
ſitions : But whoever will examine his
Poems with an impartial Eye, will find
a very deficient Plan of Morals prevail-
ing through them.   There is not the leaſt
Veſtige or Appearance of thoſe abſtract
general Principles of moral Excellence
or Blame, which take Place in the more
refined Periods of ſocial and poliſhed Life :
His Gods and Heroes fight and plunder,
kill and raviſh, boaſt and lye ; are generous, fierce, prodigal, rapacious, cruel,
or unrelenting, without much Controul
from *moral Ideas* within, or from a *refined legiſlative Art* without.

It is remarkable that PLUTARCH, after
labouring in vain through many Pages,
to prove that the Principles of all the

[x] *Qui quid pulchrum,* &c.

Virtues

Virtues are to be found in HOMER, is forced at length to conclude; " It is true, " indeed, that *bad* Actions and Principles " are intermixed and defcribed in the fame " Manner ; which was neceffary, for the " Introduction of the Sublime and Won- " derful: But this only makes the Contraft " the ftronger ; fo that the Reader is ne- " ceffarily led to *felect* the *Good* and *reject* " the *Bad* [*y*]." But as this great Ancient, along with others, allow that neither the *good* nor the *bad* is actually recommended by the Poet ; the Confequence follows, that the Reader (if fo difpofed) may as eafily *felect* the *bad*, and *reject* the *good:* That HOMER was a compleat *natural Painter* of the Ways of Men ; but an imperfect moral Painter from the *unpo-lifhed Genius* and *barbarous Legiflation* of the Age in which he lived.

The Inconfiftency of a late learned Wri-ter on this Subject is too glaring to pafs unnoticed. He juftly criticifeth VIRGIL, as being fhackled by the refined Man-ners of his Times, and the political Forms of his Country. With equal Truth he

[*y*] *In Vita* HOMERI.

difplays

difplays the free Vein of Nature, which
runs through HOMER's Poems. " The
" natural *Greek* in HOMER's Days, co-
" vered none of his Sentiments : He
" frankly owned the Pleafures of Love
" and Wine : He told how voracioufly
" he eat when he was hungry ; and how
" horribly he was frighted when he faw
" an approaching Danger : He looked on
" *no means* as *bafe* to efcape it ; and was
" not at all *afhamed* to relate the *Trick*
" or *Fetch* that had brought him off."—
" Even AGAMEMNON is not afhamed to
" own his Paffion for a captive Maid, in
" the Face of the whole Army : He tells
" them plainly, that he likes her much
" better than his Lady, the beautiful
" CLYTEMNESTRA, of the prime Gre-
" cian Nobility [z]." All this Criticifm is
juft and fine. But who can but wonder
at what follows ?—" His Work is the
" great Drama of Life acting in our
" View : *There* we fee *Virtue* and *Piety*
" *praifed* ; public *Religion promoted* ; *Tem-*
" *perance, Forgivenefs,* and Fortitude, *re-*

[z] *Enquiry into the Life and Writings of* HOMER,
p. 338.

" *warded;*

" *warded* ; Truth and Character followed ;
" and accordingly find it standing at the
" Head of human Writings [a]." As a
natural Picture of Manners, its *Superiority*
is *acknowledged* : As a *moral Picture*, its
Defects are no lefs *confpicuous.*—Where is
Virtue praifed ? Is it in the Conduct of
the natural Greek, who looked upon *no
means* as *bafe* to efcape Danger ? *Nor* was
at all *afhamed* to relate the *Trick* or *Fetch*
that brought him off ? Is it in the Conduct of AGAMEMNON, who declared his
Paffion for a *Captive*, and his *Neglect* of
his *Queen*, in the *Face* of the *whole Army* ?
—Where is *Piety* praifed ? Is it in the
Feat of DIOMEDE, who attacked and
wounded one of the Gods ?—Where is
public Religion (in the improved Senfe)
promoted ? Is it in his Defcriptions of
Heaven and *Hell*? In the *firft* of which
the *Adultery* of MARS and VENUS is
treated as a *Jeft* by all the *Gods :* In
the *fecond*, the Souls of the *beft Men* are
reprefented wandering *forlorn* and *com-
fortlefs.*

[a] *Enquiry into the Life and Writings of* HOMER,
P. 338.

In

In all this, the Poet is not blameable: He painted what he faw, and believed, and painted truly. The Fault lay in the Opinions and Manners of the Times: In the Defects of an early and barbarous Legiflation, which had but half-civilized Mankind.

Our great *Tranflator* of Homer hath often departed from the Character of his Original in this Refpect: He hath frequently thrown in fine *moral* Traits, of which there is not the leaft Footftep in his *Author*. By this, indeed, he hath given us a Poem more accommodated to the Tafte of our own Times; but hath loft the native and unpolifhed Simplicity which diftinguifhes the venerable old Prince of *Epic Song*.

The next great *legiflative Bard* whom I fhall now mention, was Pindar. At the Period when He flourifhed, the Fortune and Glory of Greece were rifing to their Meridian: The *legiflative* Arts had now obtained a higher Degree of *Perfection:* And accordingly we find, in his fublime *Songs*, the fulleft and moft perfect Union of falutary Principles, thrown out in Maxims religious, poli-

tical

tical, and moral. No Vices or Imperfections, either of Gods or Men, are there
applauded or palliated; nor ever recited,
but to be condemned: All Actions are
praifed or cenfured, according to their
Influence on the public Happinefs. The
Intent of thefe *Songs*, fung by their Author at their moſt general and renowned
Feſtivals, was to infpire his Countrymen
with the Love of Glory and of Virtue.
To this great End, he animated them,
not only by the Example and Praife of
the Victors in the *Olympic Games*; but
afcended into paſt Times, and drew from
thence the ſhining Acts of Gods and Heroes, who had diftinguiſhed themfelves by
Valour, Arts, or Virtues.

And here, in Juſtice to this great Poet
we muſt obferve, that PINDAR's Songs,
confidered in this *legiſlative* View, afford
an eafy and internal Solution of a Difficulty which hath at all Times embarraſſed his Commentators and Critics;
who have ever cenfured his feeming Ir-
regularities and fudden Flights, from the
declared Heroe of his Poem, to *Gods* and
deceafed Chieftains. But on the Principle
here given, it appears, that the Heroe of
the

the Day was but the *occaſional* and *inci-dental* Subject of his Ode.   The main Intent was the Praiſe of his Country's Gods and Heroes, who had ſignalized themſelves by Actions beneficent and great.   When therefore he ſeems to *wan-der* into the Celebration of *their* Names, he is indeed *ſeverely true* to the *leading Sub-ject* of his *Song*.

The very Objection itſelf, as it is urged by ſome of PINDAR's Critics, leads us to the Solution here given.   A French Writer thus expreſſeth it.   " He is not " always content with praiſing the *Coun-* " *try* of his *Heroe ;* he proceeds to cele- " brate the *great Men* which it had *pro-* " *duced,* and then it is that he *wanders* " *indeed.*   So when his *Heroe* is of EGINA, " after having celebrated the Iſle in *ge-* " *neral,* he deſcends to *Particulars,* and " praiſeth ÆACUS, PELEUS, TELAMON, " ACHILLES, and NEOPTOLEMUS, AJAX, " and TEUCER, who all *ſprung* from " *thence :* He mentions CYPRUS, SALA- " MINE, PHTHIA, EPIRUS, which were " *Colonies founded by theſe Heroes* [*b*]."

[*b*] *Hiſt. de l'Acad. Royale des Inſcrip.* t. v. p. 96.

There

There cannot be a better Illuftration of the *Solution* here given, than this very *Objection* thus prefented at large.

There is a fabulous Story told, which ftrongly confirms the Principle here delivered; and proves it to have been the Opinion of ancient GREECE, that a Part of thefe feftal Celebrations was due to the Gods and Heroes ; and that it was even a *Crime* to *omit* their Praifes. " The Poet " SIMONIDES, having agreed with an *Olym-* " *pic Victor*, called SCOPAS, for an Ode of " Celebration ; SIMONIDES, according to " Cuftom, went largely into the Praife of " CASTOR and POLLUX. On this, SCOPAS " gave him the *third Part* of the Price, " and told him, that he muft apply to " CASTOR and POLLUX for the Remainder. " SCOPAS being afterwards at a Banquet " with SIMONIDES, Word was brought, " that *two Men*, covered with Sweat and " Duft were at the Door, and defired to " fpeak with SIMONIDES : He went out " of the Chamber, and immediately the " Roof fell in, and buried SCOPAS in " the Ruins [c]."

[c] CICERO *de Oratore*, l. ii. QUINTIL. l. xi. c. 2.

F　　　　　　　　　The

The three *Greek* TRAGEDIANS are the laft of this illuftrious Catalogue of legiflative Bards: And their Writings, though very different in their Style and Manner, yet all unite in holding forth the leading Principles of the Greek Religion, Polity, and Morals.

ESCHYLUS, who ftands firft in Order of Time, partakes much of the rude Genius of the early Periods. His Imagery and Sentiments are great; his Style rugged and abrupt; and of a Caft fo totally different from that of HOMER, that it is aftonifhing to hear the Critics, one after another, affirming that HOMER was his Model [*d*]. His Writings prefent to us all the Characters of a fublime, original, and uncultivated Genius, which fcorned any other Tutorefs than *Nature.* He was himfelf a great Warrior; and his warlike Genius threw itfelf out, in Subjects that were grand and terrible. Hence his Tragic Songs abound with the moft gloomy and tremendous Exploits of the Grecian Heroes, ftriking the Soul with Admiration, Aftonifhment, and Terror.

[*d*] See this Point confidered below, Art. 18.

SOPHO

SOPHOCLES appeared next; of a more
fedate and tempered Majefty : He improved on ESCHYLUS both in *Plan* and
Morals. For the *legiflative Arts* were now
advancing at ATHENS with great Rapi-
dity. No Wonder, therefore, that the
Difciple conquered his Mafter ; when he
had the improving Senfe of his Country
to elevate and inlarge his Genius. But '
ftill the Gods and Heroes of GREECE
were the conftant Subjeƈt of his Song.

EURIPIDES, confidered in the legiflative View, was on a Level with his Mafters with Refpeƈt to the Subjeƈt of his
Tragedies (for thefe were always drawn
from the *Grecian Gods* or *Heroes*) but
poffeffed himfelf of the Advantage which
the ftill improving State of his Country
gave him. For *Philofophy* was now in its
Afcendant : The *Poet* was the *Difciple* of
an eminent *Sage* : Hence the Genius of
EURIPIDES carried the legiflative Power
of Song to its laft Perfeƈtion ; and threw
itfelf out in fuch a Variety of Maxims,
political and *moral*, as far outwent the
Art of his Predeceffors.

Such then, through the various Ages
of ancient GREECE, was the legiflative

Genius

Genius of their *Songs ;* which, in their
feveral Periods contained the leading Principles of their *Religion, Morals,* and *Polity;*
and thus became the natural and proper
Object of the public Attention and Regard.

10. " MUSIC, in its more extenfive
" Meaning, that is, including *Melody* and
" *poetic Song* [*e*] either with or without
" the *Dance*" (for this laft, as will appear
below [*f*], was foon feparated from the
other two, for an important End) " bore
" a principal and effential Part in the Edu-
" cation of their Children." The Authorities which prove this are abundant, and
even fuperfluous. Some of the principal
may fuffice. " Among the Ancients" (fays
the wife PLUTARCH) " Mufic in Theatres
" was not known : They employed all
" their Art in the Worfhip of the Gods,
" and the Education of their Youth [*g*]."
The fame Author gives feveral Inftances
of Mufical Education in CRETE and
SPARTA ; and tells us, that " By Mufic
" the young Men were taught to *abftain*
" from every thing *indecent* in *Word* and
" *Deed;* and to obferve *Decorum, Tempe-*

[*e*] See above, Art. 1.   [*f*] See Art. 12.
[*g*] PLUT. *de Mufica.*

" *rance,*

" *rance*, and Regularity [*h*]." Again: " Mu-
" fic was the Foundation of a virtuous Edu-
" cation; becaufe it was allied with *Phi-*
" *lofophy, Morals*, and *Heroifm*: ACHILLES
" was taught by CHIRON, and played
" and fung the *great Actions* of *Heroes* [*i*]."
Elfewhere he informs us, that " the *Spar-*
" *tans* in their *Songs* talked high of what
" *Exploits* they had performed: And that
" the *young Men* echoed back their *Tri-*
" *umphs* in their Songs, proclaiming their
" Refolution to *equal* the Valour of their
" *Forefathers* [*k*]."

Such was the Nature of ancient *Mufic*
when applied to Education; and not a
mere Proficiency in the *playing* or *finging*
Art, as it hath been generally mifunder-
ftood, and ignorantly ridiculed by many
Moderns. Hence it was, that their greateft
Captains and Statefmen ftudied Mufic, as
an effential Part of Education. Thus PE-
RICLES was taught by DAMON, who was
likewife fuppofed to have inftructed him
in Politics [*l*]. Thus EPAMINONDAS was
eminent in Mufic; though the *Roman* Hi-

[*h*] PLUT. *de Mufica.*   [*i*] Ibid.   [*k*] *In Lycurgo.*
[*l*] PLUT. *in Pericle.*

ftorian [*m*], who informs us of the Fact, fpeaks like one who knew not the Nature and Extent of Mufic among the earlier Greeks.

PLATO confirms thefe Authorities; and recites more at large the particular Method of Education ufed in ancient GREECE. " What then is the moft proper Difcipline? " Will it not be difficult to find a better, " than what was long ago eftablifhed? One " Part of this is the *Gymnaftic*, which relates " to the *Body*; the other is *Mufic*, which " relates to the *Mind*. This Difcipline ought " firft to begin with *Mufic*; and when we " fpeak of *Mufic*, we include the *Subject*, " *Words*, or *Song*. Of this there are two " Kinds, the *true* and *fabulous*. Both " ought to be applied; but the fabulous " firft. Yet the *Fables* ought to be *regu-* " *lated*, left the young Mind being tinctured " with fuch as are improper, it fhould be " neceffary at a more adult Age to counter- " work the firft Impreffions [*n*]." He then proceeds to a particular Detail of Fables proper and improper in the Work of Edu- cation, pointing out what ought to be ad-

[*m*] CORN. *Nepos in Præfat. Vit.* EPAMINOND.
[*n*] *De Repub.* l. ii.

mitted

mitted or rejected.   In another Dialogue,
he fpeaks again of the Remains of this
Method of Inftruction, which were found
among the wifer Sort, even in his own
Times; although in general (as will appear
below [*o*]) *Mufic* was then totally *corrupted.*
" The Parents commit their Children to the
" Care of Mafters; and are more follicitous
" about their *Morals*, than their Proficiency
" in *Learning*, or *playing* on the *Lyre*.   As
" foon as they have attained a Knowledge
" of Letters, and are able to underftand
" what they read, the Mafters give them
" the Works of the *beft Poets* to perufe and
" get by Heart, efpecially fuch as contain
" the *Praifes* of their *Forefathers* renowned
" for *great Actions*, that the Boys may be
" fired with an *Emulation* to *imitate* their
" *Virtues.*   The Mufic-Mafters are above
" all Things careful to give them Habits
" of Wifdom and Temperance, and to fee
" that they commit no unworthy Action.
" As foon as they have learnt to play on
" the Lyre, the Mafter proceeds to inftruct
" them in the *Songs* of the moft famous
" *Poets:* Thefe they *fing* to the Lyre; and

[*o*] Art. 34, 35.

F 4   " the

" the Preceptors endeavour to bring their
" Boys to a Love of the Rythms and Num-
" bers; that by this Difcipline they may
" be more *mild, modeft,* and *orderly* in their
" *Manners,* and become *ufeful* both in
" *Speech* and *Action* [*p*]."

Suitable to this Method of Education is
PLATO's Direction in his Book of Laws.
" Therefore the Legiflator will take Care,
" that the Youth's Mind may be fo formed,
" that his *Pleafures* and *Difpleafures* may
" *accord* to the *Laws,* and to the Tafte of
" *mature Age:* And if it be neceffary, he
" will compel the Poet to defcribe the *Ac-*
" *tions* of *brave* and *good* Men; and to com-
" pofe fuch *Numbers* and *Harmonies* as may
" be fuited to the Subjects [*q*]."

In the fame Place he affigns a particular
Reafon for this Method of Education:
" Becaufe the youthful Mind is not apt to
" attend to ferious Study, therefore the
" *pleafing Vehicle* of *Song* is to be admini-
" ftered [*r*]." He then proceeds even to
the particular moral Maxims which ought
to be inftilled by the Poet and Mufi-

[*p*] *In Protag.*   [*q*] *De Legibus,* l. ii.   [*r*] Ibid.

cian,

,cian, on the Principles of a wife Legiflator.

As thefe Authorities are clear and decifive, we may here properly obviate an
Error of the excellent MONTESQUIEU,
arifing from his Mifapprehenfion of the
true Nature and Extent of ancient Mufic.
He, with moft other Writers, fuppofeth
it to have confifted (according to the modern Acceptation of the Word) in the
fingle Circumftance of *Melody*. In Confequence of this, when he comes to inquire
why the ancient *Greeks* applied Mufic fo
univerfally in the Education of their Children, he fays, " As they were a warlike
" People, and therefore in Danger of de-
" generating into a favage Ferocity of
" Manners, they employed Mufic, as the
" beft Means of foftening their Tempers
" into a milder Character ; and this, be-
" caufe Mufic, of all the Pleafures of
" Senfe, has the leaft Tendency to cor-
" rupt the Soul [s]." And fo far, indeed,
is true, that the ancient Greeks did confider this as one of the falutary Effects
arifing from the Application of Mufic [t].

[s] *L'Efprit des Loix*, l. iv. c. 8.
[t] PLATO *de Rep*. l. iii.

But

But we now find that the Matter lay much deeper: That Mufic, in its ancient Senfe, implied not only *Melody* but *Verfe* or *Song* : That it was the *eftablifhed Vehicle* of all the leading *Principles* of their *Religion*, *Morals*, and *Polity* ; and therefore was the natural and moft important Inftrument or Mean in the Education of their Children.

The learned DACIER falls into the fame Error, with Refpect to the wonderful Efficacy of *Mufic*, in the *Education* of the *Arcadians*, and the fatal Want of it among the Inhabitants of CYNÆTHE, as the Fact is recorded by POLÝBIUS and ATHENÆUS. " If (fays the Critic) POLYBIUS
" fpeaks thus of *Mufic*, and if he accufeth
" EPHORUS of having advanced a thing
" unworthy of him, in faying that this
" Art was invented to deceive Mankind;
" what may we not fay of *Tragedy*, of
" which *Mufic* is but a *fmall Ornament*,
" and which as far furpaffeth *Mufic*, as
" *Speech* is beyond inarticulate and *un-*
" *meaning Sounds* [*u*]." In this Paffage, the learned Writer . evidently fuppofes

[*u*] DACIER *Poët. d'Ariftote. Preface.*

that

that the ancient *Muſic*, which wrought
ſuch Wonders in the Education of the
Arcadians, was no more than mere *Melody* or *unmeaning Sound*. But the Account
which both POLYBIUS and ATHENÆUS
give of the muſical Education of the *Arcadians*, confirms all that hath been here
advanced; and proves, that it conſiſted
in the Application of the united Powers
of *Dance, Melody*, and *Song*.

The moſt learned VOSSIUS proceeds on
the ſame Miſtake in his firſt Book *De
Natura Artium* : And continues under
the Influence of this fundamental Error,
through his whole Diſſertation on *Muſic*.
As it may ſeem unaccountable, how ſo
capital a Miſtake ſhould creep into the
Writings of theſe great Authors, let me
here obſerve, as an Apology for them all,
that ARISTOTLE, and ſome ſucceeding
Writers, ſpeak of *Muſic* as an Art *diſtinct*
from *Poetry* [w] : It was therefore natural
enough for theſe Writers to draw their
Ideas of ancient Muſic from the great
Maſter-Critic of GREECE. How it came
to paſs, that ARISTOTLE ſhould ſpeak

[w] *Poët paſſim.*

of

of thefe Arts as *two*, which the elder Writers confidered as *one*, will clearly appear below [*x*]; where we fhall fee, that in the Time of Aristotle, a Separation of the *Melody* and *poetic Song* had taken Place ; that the firft retained the Name of *Mufic*, and the fecond affumed that of *Poetry*.

11. "Music—that is, *Melody, Dance*, " and *poetic Song*, thus *united*,—acquired a " *great* and *general Power* over the Minds " and Actions of the ancient *Greeks*." It is prefumed, that we have now gained an Afcent, from whence this Truth will appear evident and indifputable ; though it hath long been regarded by many, as an incredible Paradox.—How, or whence, fuch an univerfal Paffion for Mufic fhould have arifen in Greece; or, after it had arifen, how it gained fuch a general Eftablifhment in the important Article of Education; or, after it was thus eftablifhed, how it could work fuch mighty Effects upon the Mind, fuppofing it to confift only in mere *Melody* ; —are Queftions which wife Men have afked, and Bigots to Antiquity have weakly anfwered : For the common Reply hath

[*x*] Art. 35.

been,

been, that their *Mufic* (meaning their *Melody)* was of a Kind fo much fuperior to
ours, that all its wonderful Effects followed from its more exalted Nature.——
On the contrary, it appears, that as to
its particular Conftruction, we are ignorant of it : That we have no precife or
practicable Idea of their *Genera,* their
Modes; nor the *Make,* nor *Power* of their
Inftruments : But by collateral Arguments
we can prove that their *Melody* was fomething altogether *fimple* and *inartificial;* becaufe it was fuch as Statefmen, Warriors,
and Bards, occupied in other Purfuits,
could compofe; and fuch as high and
low, Children and Men bufied in other
concerns of Life, could learn and practife.
Hence we are led to believe, that whatever
Effects arofe from the mere *Melody,* arofe
from its *Rythm* or *Meafure,* heightened by
early *Affociation* and continued *Habit;* by
which it became a Kind of natural *Language* of the Paffions [*y*]. It appears farther, that *Melody* formed but a *Part* of
the ancient *Mufic;* and that its moft im-

[*y*] For the particular Proof of all that relates to
the *Melody* of the ancient *Greeks,* fee the *Differtation on
Poetry and Mufic.*   Sect. v. p. 62, &c.

portant

portant and effential Branch was that of
Verfe or *Song*.   But for a clear and full
View of the Origin and Union of their
Melody and *poetic Song*, it was neceffary to
go back, 'and begin our Inquiries at the
early Period of favage Life, in which all
the Seeds and Principles of civilized Society
appear in their native and uncultivated
State. This Method of Inyeftigation hath
opened to us an involved and clouded
Subject.   Hence it appears, that *Melody*,
Dance, and *Song*, naturally arofe in *Union;*
that *Meafure*, *Rythm*, and *Numbers*, were
the certain Confequence : That in the
earlieft Times of GREECE, the Characters
of *Legiflator* and *Bard* did often and naturally *coalefce :* That hence their earlieft
Hiftories, *Laws*, and *Oracles*, were of courfe
written in *Verfe ;* that their religious
Rites were naturally, and without pofitive
Appointment, performed or accompanied
by Melody, Dance, and poetic Song :
That through the feveral improving Periods of Time, their Songs were more and
more of a true legiflative Caft ; that they
included all the great Actions of their
Gods and Heroes, and that in thefe were
contained the leading Principles of their
                                                    Reli-

Religion, Morals, and Polity : That *Mufic*, in this its inlarged Senfe, bore an effential and principal Part in the Education of their Children ; being the pleafing and powerful Vehicle, by which all the important Precepts of Life were inftilled into their tender Minds.—Thus naturally *Poem* and *Melody* arofe in Union, and were *powerfully eftablifhed* in ancient GREECE : And from this View of their Nature and Eftablifhment, their *general Influence* muft unavoidably follow : " For through the " Force of early and continued Habit, " together with the irrefiftible Contagion " of public Example maintained by the " general Practice of the whole Commu- " nity, who had received the fame Im- " preffions in their infant State ; and " while every thing pleafing, great, and " important, was conveyed through this " Medium ; fuch ftrong Affociations did " ftrike themfelves into the Tribes of " GREECE, as naturally produced the " moft lafting Effects, and fuch as no " future Incidents of Life could eafily " weaken or efface."

On thefe Principles we may naturally explain fome of the recorded Effects of

·*ancient*

ancient Mufic, which according to the common Interpretation of the Word, have been liable to the Derifion of modern Critics.

We read, that fuch was the Power of ancient Mufic, that when AGAMEMNON went to TROY, the defigning EGISTHUS could not debauch CLITEMNESTRA, till he had decoyed away the *Mufician* that was retained in the Palace. This Account, if we underftand by *Mufic* no more than *Melody*, hath much the Air of Hyperbole and Fable. But if we regard the *Mufician* as what indeed he was, the Difpenfer of *religious* and *moral* Principles, and that he urged the great Duty of conjugal Fidelity with the united Powers of poetic Eloquence and Song; and urged them to one whofe Education had made her fufceptible of fuch Impreffions; the fabulous Appearances diffolve; and we fee, that no other Method could have been devifed, fo effectual for the Prefervation of a weak Woman's Virtue.

Again; we are told, that certain young Men heated with Wine, had agreed to affault the Doors of a modeft Woman, and abufe her as a Proftitute: but that an able Mufician coming paft, he fung and

and played to them in the *Dorian* Mode;
on which they were ſtruck with Shame,
and defiſted from their Enterprize [z].
This, to modern Comprehenſion, hath ſtill
more the Air of Fable : But when the Faƈt
is well explained, the Ridicule vaniſheth
with the Myſtery.   For every *different*
Subjeƈt had a *different Mode* annexed to it.
This appears at large from PLATO. " You
" muſt adapt the Mode to the Subjeƈt and
" Words, not theſe to the Mode or Har-
" mony : On theſe Matters we will farther
" deliberate with DAMON, what Feet or
" Meaſures are fitteſt to expreſs Illibera-
" lity, Petulance, frantic Folly, and other
" Vices ; and what Meaſures beſt expreſs
" their contrary Virtues. *Hence* it is, that
" Rythm and Numbers gain their Power
" in the muſical Education, and exerciſe
" their mighty Influence on the Paſſions
" of the Soul [a]."   Tis plain, therefore, when the Hiſtorian tells us, that
the Muſician conquered the young De-
bauchees by an Application of the *Do-*

[z] This Story is ridiculed in the *Memoirs* of MAR-
TINUS SCRIBLERUS : And the Ridicule is founded on
an entire Miſapprehenſion or Miſrepreſentation, of the
true Nature of *ancient* MUSIC.

[a] *De Repub.* l. iii.

G   *rian*

rian Mode, he means to fignify, that
the Melody was accompanied by a *poetic
Exhortation* fuited to the Numbers; and
this could be no other than a Leffon of
Modefty and *Temperance*; which being conveyed by the pleafing Vehicle of Melody
and Song, addreffed to thofe who by the
Tenor of their Education muft feel its
Force, and given by one whofe Profeffion
they had been taught to reverence, could
hardly fail of its defigned Effects, unlefs
their Intemperance had prevented all Attention.

There are other recorded Effects of ancient Mufic of a fimilar Nature, which it
is not neceffary to produce here, becaufe
they may all be accounted for on the fame
Principle. With Refpect to the traditionary
Influence of this Art on *wild Beafts,
Stocks,* and *Stones,* as it came down from
the ignorant and fabulous Times, fo nothing can be juftly concluded from it,
but the Force of *Mufic* over the Minds of
uninftructed and wondering *Barbarians.*

Thus the boafted Power of the ancient
Greek Poem and *Melody* feems naturally
and fully accounted for. And in Confirmation of this Solution, we may finally
appeal

appeal to the favage Tribes with whom this Inquiry began. For by Means parallel in moft other Refpects, fave only in the Article of Legiflation and Letters, they animate each other by the early and continued Ufe of Melody, Dance, and Song, to Valour in Arms, to Conftancy in Torments and Death [*b*]. This is found, in Fact, to be an Education of fuch mighty Influence, that the *War-Song* and *Death-Song* infpire whole Tribes with a Degree of *Fury* and *Indurance*, which hath become the Aftonifhment of all who have *feen* but never *felt* their Power.

SECT V.

Of the Progreffions of Poetry in ancient Greece.

THE Origin, Nature, and Power, of the ancient Greek *Poem* and *Melody* being thus explained ; let us now proceed to a like Application of the remaining Articles of the third Section ; in which we fhall endeavour to unfold the various *Progreffions* of this Art in

[*b*] LAFITAU, tom. iii. p. 171. tom. iv. p. 9.

GREECE,

GREECE, and purfue it through its feveral Advances towards *Perfection*, to its
final *Corruption* and *Decay*.

12. " The *Dance* was feparated from the
" *Poem* or *Song* ; and with or without
" *Melody* became itfelf a diftinct Exercife
" or Art, under the Title of *Gymnaftic*, for
" the Sake of increafing their Strength and
" Agility of Body, as the Means of ren-
" dering them invincible in War." This
was the natural Effect of their warlike
Character, for the Reafon given above [*c*].
And that this was the real Generation of
the *Gymnaftic* Art, appears evidently from
PLATO's Book of *Laws* : where, having
fpoken of the three conftituent Parts of
a compleat *Choir* (Melody, Dance, and
Song) he proceeds to deduce from thefe
the Origin of the *Gymnaftic* Art. " Is not
" this the leading Principle of the *Gym-*
" *naftic* Art, that every Creature is born
" with a natural Inclination to leap or
" bound ? But Man being endowed with
" a Senfe of *Rythm* or *Numbers*, naturally
" formed his Motions into *Dance : Melody*
" naturally begets *Rythm ;* and thefe two

[*c*] See Sect. iii. Art. 12.

" *united*

" *united* form the *Gymnaſtic.*—For *That* we
" call the *Gymnaſtic,* when the *Dance* is
" ſo artificially applied, as to improve
" the Powers of the Body [*d*]." That
this Art was applied by the ancient *Greeks*
to the End of public and warlike Service,
is generally known : However, if it needs
a Proof, another Paſſage of the ſame Author will ſufficiently confirm it. " After
" theſe Inſtructions (in *Muſic*) the Parents
" ſend their Sons to the Maſters of the
" *Gymnaſtic* Schools, that by gaining a
" firm Habit of Body, which may ſecond
" a well-formed Mind, they may be able
" to indure the Toils of *Enterpriſe* and
" *War* [*e*]."

We trace the Foundation and Progreſs
of the *Gymnaſtic* Art no leſs clearly in
LUCIAN's Account. " The *Spartans,* hav-
" ing received this Art (of Dancing) from
" CASTOR and POLLUX, went *dancing* to
" *Battle,* to the Sound of Flutes : Their
" Application to Muſic did not leſſen their
" Attention to Arms : For a Muſician ſat
" in the midſt of the Aſſembly, and play-
" ed on the Flute, beating Time with his

[*d*] *De Leg.* l. ii.   [*e*] *In Protag.*

G 3   " Foot;

" Foot ; while they regularly followed
" the Meafure, in a Variety of warlike
" Poftures [*f*]."

To confirm thefe Evidences, we may
add another Inftance of a warlike *Dance,*
which approacheth neareft to the Eftablifhment of the *Gymnaftic* Exercife, of any
recorded by Antiquity. XENOPHON, in
his " Expedition of CYRUS," defcribes one
of thefe Dances in the following Manner.
" The *Feaft* being ended, the *Libations*
" made, and the *Hymn* fung, two *Thraci-*
" *ans,* completely armed, began to dance
" to the Sound of the Flute : After fkir-
" ihifhing for fome time with their Swords,
" one of them (as wounded) fell down,
" on which the *Paphlagonians* fet up a
" loud Cry. The Conqueror having ftrip-
" ped his Adverfary, departed finging his
" Victory."—Here we fee a near Approach
to the Forms of the *Gymnaftic* Exercife in
their moft effential Circumftances, yet the
original Form of the *Dance* remains.

Thus the Origin of the *Gymnaftic* Arts
is clearly unfolded, as being no more
than a Part of the favage *Song-Feaft ;*

[*f*] *D: Saltatione.*

but

but feparated from thence for the Ends
of warlike Service.   For Want of this
Information, the learned Vossius, among
other Authors, ftiles the *Dance* a Branch
of the *Gymnaftic*, inftead of regarding the
Gymnaftic as the Offspring of the *Dance* [*g*].

Here we may farther obferve, that this
View of the *Gymnaftic*, confidered as having been originally a Branch of the *Mufical* Art, clears up a Difficulty with which
every other Account of it is encumbered.
Thus a late Writer fays, " The Exercife
" of *leaping* in the *Pentathlon* was accom-
" panied by *Flutes*, playing *Pythian* Airs,
" as Pausanias informs us. Whence this
" Cuftom was derived, I cannot fay: And
" the Reafon affigned for it by that Au-
" thor, which is certainly not the true one,
" may induce us to think, that in this
" Matter the Ancients were as ignorant as
" we [*h*]." But on the Principle here given,
the Cuftom accounts for itfelf.   In the firft
Inftitution of the *Gymnaftic* Arts, it appears
that *Melody* made a *Part* of them: This
Part had been difufed (by Courfe of

[*g*] *De Nat. Art.* l. i. c. 3.
[*h*] West's *Tranfl. of* Pindar's *Odes: Pref.*

G 4   Time)

Time) in the *other* Exercifes, but had been retained in that of *Leaping* in the *Pentathlon.*

13. "After a certain Period of Civili-
"zation, the *complex* Character of *Legif-*
"*lator* and *Bard* did *feparate,* and were
"feldom united." This Separation, it hath been fhewn above, would of Courfe follow from decreafing Enthufiafm, and the increafing Labours of Government. And fuch was the natural Rife of the αοιδοι or *Bards* of ancient GREECE: Of whofe *Pro-*
feffion and *Art* a late learned Author [i] hath in many Circumftances, though not in all, given a juft Idea. Of its original Dignity and Importance, in the moft ancient Times, he did not rightly conceive; through his Ignorance of its true Rife, and original Union with the Legiflator's Office. He reprefents them as wandering Muficians only, who were *welcome* to the Houfes of the *Great.* Such indeed they were, in the *later* Periods; when the Separation had been long formed, and their Office become rather an Affair of *Amufe-*
ment than *Utility.* But as in the earlieft

[i] *Enquiry into the Life and Writings of* HOMER.

Periods

Periods the *Legiflators* themfelves were often *Bards*, fo when the Separation of Character was firft made, the known Influence and Importance of their Office could
make them no other than *Affiftants* to the
Magiftrate, in the high Tafk of govern-
ing the People. Of this we have a clear
Inftance in the Commonwealth of SPARTA
(which maintained all its original Infti-
tutions the moft pure and unchanged)
where a dangerous Infurrection arofe ;
nor could be quelled by the Magiftrate,
till the Bard TERPANDER came, and
played and fung at their public Place of
Congrefs [*k*].

HESIOD, who was himfelf of this Order, hath given us a noble Defcription
of their Office and Dignity : Which, as
it ftrongly confirms the Genealogy here
given, I fhall tranflate at large ; together
with his Picture of the *Magiftrate* ; along
with whom the *Bard* appears to co-operate
in the public Welfare, as the *fecond* Character in the *Community*. " Therefore Kings
" (Magiftrates) are watchful, that they may
" do Juftice to the Injured, at the Place of

[*k*] SUIDAS, *on the Leftian Song.*

" public

" public Congrefs, foothing the Paffions
" of Men by perfuafive Speech : The Peo-
" ple reverence him as a God, while he
" paffes through the City.—*Kings* are from
" JOVE : *Bards* are from the *Mufes* and the
" far-fhooting APOLLO. Happy is He
" whom the Mufes love : His Lips flow
" with fweet and foothing Accents. If any
" hath a keen and inward Grief, frefh-
" rankling in his Soul ; the Bard, the
" Mufes Minifter, no fooner fings the
" Praife of *ancient Heroes*, and the *Gods*
" who inhabit OLYMPUS, than he forgets
" his Sorrows, and feels no more his An-
" guifh.—Hail, Daughters of JOVE ! In-
" fpire *Me* with your perfuafive Song [*l*]."

It feems probable that the original *Dignity* of the *Bard's* Character was always
maintained longer in *Commonwealths* than
under defpotic or *kingly* Governments :
For at the Court of ALCINOUS, fo early
as the Age of HOMER's Heroes, it appears, from the Picture given of DEMO-
DOCUS, to have funk into a Character of
Dependance [*m*]. The Reafon is manifeft :
The *Republican* Form fubfifts by an united

[*l*] HES. THEOG.   [*m*] *Odyff.*

Exertion

Exertion of the Powers of every Rank: Under the *despotic* Rule, the Influence of thefe various Powers is fwallowed up in the abfolute Will of ONE. We fhall fee the Bard's Character rifing again in its dignified State, in the early Periods of other barbarous Nations [*n*].

14. " In the Courfe of Time, and Pro-
" grefs of Polity and Arts, a *Separation* of
" the feveral *Kinds* of *Song* did arife. In
" the early Periods they lay confufed; and
" were mingled in the fame Compofition,
" as Inclination, Enthufiafm, or other In-
" cidents might impel."—This Fact is ma-
nifeft enough, from the Catalogue already given of the Writings of the moft an-
cient Bards of GREECE ; for by this it appears, that they ranged at large through the Fields of Poetry and *Song*, without giving any precife or legitimate Form to their Compofitions ; which feem moft gene-
rally to have been a rapturous Mixture of *Hymn, Hiftory, Fable,* and *Mythology,* thrown out by the enthufiaftic Bard in legiflative Songs, as different Motives or Occafions prefented themfelves, and ac-

[*n*] See below, Sect. vii.

cording to the Exigencies or Capacity of his furrounding Audience.—" But repeat- " ed Trial and Experiment produced a " more artificial Manner ; and thus by " Degrees, the feveral Kinds of Poem af- " fumed their legitimate Forms."—For the Truth of this, we refer to the following Articles.

15. " HYMNs and *Odes* were compofed, " and *fung* by their Compofers at their " feftal Solemnities." This Species of Song hath, in the Way of Prehemi- nence, and beyond any other, gained the Title of *lyric Poetry*. Nor can we wonder at this, if we confider, that from its Nature it muft have arifen firft, muft have been firft moulded into Form, and muft, from its peculiar Genius, con- tinue united with *Melody* longer and more univerfally than any other. It arofe firft, becaufe it was natural for the favage Mind, to throw itfelf out in fudden Exclamations of Grief or Joy, Love, Revenge, or Anguifh, before it could find Means or Leifure to recite at large the Occafions of thefe powerful Feel- ings : It muft be firft moulded into Form, becaufe its Extent is the fmalleft, and its

Plan

Plan moſt ſimple : It muſt continue united
with *Melody* longer and more univerſally
than any other Species, becauſe the very
Eſſence of its Subject is that which the
other Kinds only catch incidentally, I
mean, the ſudden Shocks and Emotions
of the Soul ; which are found to be the
powerful Bands of Nature, by which *Melody*
and *Song* are moſt cloſely bound together.

PLUTARCH confirms this Reaſoning
concerning the *Priority* of the *hymnal* Species ; and ſays, that " Muſic was *firſt* uſed
" in religious Ceremonies, being employed
" in the *Praiſes* of the *Gods* ; and that af-
" terwards it was applied to *other* Sub-
" jects [*o*]." Accordingly we find, that in
the ſeveral ſucceſſive Periods, ALCÆUS,
STESICHORUS, TYRTÆUS, and others,
compoſed and ſung their *Odes* at the
public Feſtivals. The ſublime PINDAR
was not more celebrated for his mighty
Strains, than for his powerful Performance of them at the *Olympic Games :*
Nay, ſo high was his Fame in this Regard, that he had a Chair appropriated to
him in the Temple of DELPHI, where
he poured forth the Torrent of his

[*o*] *De Muſica.*

Songs,

Songs, which were attended to, and re
vered as Oracles issuing from the Inspira-
tion of the God.

16. "The *Epic* Poem arose ; and was
"sung by its Composers at their festal
"Solemnities."—When the first Fire of
Enthusiasm had vented itself in the Rapture of *Hymns* and *Odes*, it naturally af-
sumed a more *sedate* Manner ; and found
Time to *relate* at large those Actions which
in it's first Agitations it could only celebrate by sudden Bursts of Passion and
Praise. Accordingly, we find many of
the elder Poets of GREECE mixing the
hymnal and *enthusiastic* with the *historic* or
narrative Species. The Exploits of BAC-
CHUS, the Rape of PROSERPINE, the
Wars of the TITANS, were among their
favourite Themes. After these, came the
Authors of the *Herculiad* and *Thesiad :*
DEMODOCUS, prior to HOMER, sung the
Ambush of the *Trojan Horse :* PHEMIUS
sung the Return of the *Greeks* under AGA-
MEMNON : The *little Iliad* comprised most
of the subsequent Adventures of the *Trojan War.* A *Thebaid* was also written,
the Author of which is not certainly
known ; though PAUSANIAS tell us, it
was

was by many afcribed to HOMER [*p*]. As Example, Habit, and improving Arts and Polity, are the neceffary Means of Progrefs in every Art, fo thefe Accounts, though imperfectly conveyed to us (becaufe the Poems they allude to are loft) fufficiently imply, that the *Epic* Mufe advanced *gradually* towards Perfection; till at length fhe appeared in full Splendor, in the Perfon of her favoured HOMER.

HERODOTUS, indeed, has thrown out a Hint, as if the *Iliad* was prior to the oldeft of the Poems afcribed to thefe moft ancient Bards [*q*]. VELLEIUS PATERCULUS affirms the fame thing in ftronger Terms [*r*]: And Mr. POPE goes into this Opinion [*s*]. It muft be confeffed, the Hiftory of thefe remote Ages is fo dark and fabulous, that nothing can with Certainty be collected from them. But the very Structure of HOMER's Poem carries in itfelf fuch an internal Evidence, as turns the Scale againft the Hiftorian's Conjecture. If we confider the Nature of the human Mind, we fhall be led to be-

[*p*] L. ix.   [*q*] *In* EUTERPE.   [*r*] L. i. c. 5.
[*s*] Diff. prefixed to his Tranf. of the *Iliad*.

lieve,

lieve, that the *Epic* Poem muſt have received a *gradual* Improvement through
that long though unknown Tract of Time,
during which its unpoliſhed Rudiments
exiſted before the Age of HOMER. The
mere Powers of *Fancy* and *Execution*
may, indeed, arrive at their higheſt Perfection by the Efforts of a *ſingle Mind:*
For what belongs to Nature only, Nature
only can complete; and thus our immortal SHAKESPEAR aroſe: But that an *Epic*
PLAN, ſo *complex,* ſo *vaſt,* and yet ſo *perfect* as that of the *Iliad;* which requires
an uncommon Penetration even to comprehend in all its Variety and Art; which
the thoughtful, the literate, the poliſhed
VIRGIL attempted to rival, and only
proved his utter Inability by his Attempt;
which ſucceeding Poets have made their
Model, yet none have ever equalled or
approached, ſave only the all-compre-
hending Mind of the ſublime MILTON;
—that ſuch a Plan as This, which re-
quired the higheſt Efforts of an improved
Underſtanding, opened and ſtrengthened
by a Succeſſion of preceding Examples,
ſhould at once emerge in all the Extent
of Art, in the midſt of rude and unformed
Fables,

Fables, fung at Feftivals as vague Enthufiafm might infpire ;—this is an Opinion
repugnant to all our Notices concerning
the Progrefs of the Powers of the human
Mind. We may as rationally fuppofe that
St. PAUL's was the firft built Temple,
its *Organ* the firft mufical Inftrument, the
LAOCOON and his Sons the firft Attempt
in Statuary, the *Transfiguration* the firft
Effay in Picture, as that the *ftupendous
Iliad,* the Wonder of all fucceeding Ages,
was the *firft* Attempt in *Epic* Poetry.

What the Nature of the Thing fo
ftrongly declares, ARISTOTLE feems to
confirm in his Poetics : For he fays, that
" although we know not the Names ei-
" ther of the Poems or their Authors ;
" yet there is Reafon to believe that many
" had been written before HOMER ; and
" that his *Margites* brought this Species
" to its Perfection, in the fame Manner
" as the *Iliad* and *Odyffy* had compleated
" the Form of the Epic Poem [*t*]."

We may reafonably conclude, therefore,
that from the Days of LINUS, down to
thofe of HOMER, there had been a Suc-

[*t*] *Poet.* c. iv.

H   ceffion

ceffion of Writers, among whom the Form
of the *Epic* Poem had been *gradually* advancing towards Perfection, till it received
its full Completion in the Birth of the *Iliad.*

That thefe Epic Songs, in their feveral
Periods, were fung by their Compofers to
the furrounding People, we have the general Teftimony of ancient Writers. This
Fact is fo clear, with Refpect to the elder
Poets of GREECE, that it is queftioned
by fome whether ever their *Songs* were
committed to *Writing :* Whether they were
any more than the extempore Efforts of
a fudden Enthufiafm, kindled by the fym-
pathetic Power of *religious Rites,* or *State-
Feftivals.* That HOMER followed the honourable Profeffion of a *Bard,* and fung
his own Poems at the public Feafts, hath
been proved at large by a learned Writer [*u*]. HESIOD was of the fame Order;
and feems to have maintained it with truer
Dignity [*w*]. TERPANDER held the fame
Employment, and fung both his own
Poems and thofe of HOMER [*x*].

17. " From an *Union* of thefe two Kinds,
" a certain rude Outline of *Tragedy* arofe."

[*u*] *Life* of HOMER, Sect. vii, viii.   [*w*] THEOG.
Exord. ver. 23, &c.   [*x*] PLUTARCH *de Mufica.*

—For

—For when a Bard fung the great or terrible Atchievements of a Heroe or God,
the furrounding *Audience*, fired to Enthufiafm, and already prepared by a correfpondent Education, would naturally break
forth into the Raptures of a *choral Song*.
—This Progreffion of Poetry is fo natural, that it is Matter of Aftonifhment to
hear the Learned at all Times afcribing
the Rife of Tragedy to Caufes merely accidental ; and confining it to the fingle
Adventure of THESPIS and his Route,
finging the Praifes of BACCHUS at a
cafual Vintage. Thus DACIER, among
others, affirms roundly, that " the firft
" dramatic Perfon which THESPIS *in-*
" *vented*, was only *defigned* to give Refpite
" to the Choir ; and what he recited was
" no more than an Appendage to Tra-
" gedy [y]." In the fame Manner the
fenfible and learned BRUMOY delivers at
large the common Syftem, with Refpect
to the Birth and Progrefs of the *tragic*
Species [z]. All this is in Contradiction
to the Workings of Nature ; and, without

[y] *Sur les Poet D'Arift.* p. 47.
[z] *Theat. des Grecs,* tom. vi. p. 310, &c.

H 2   Proof,

Proof, fuppofes That to be a *cafual Inven-*
tion in a *particular* Inftance, which was
indeed the *natural Progrefs* of Paffion expreffed by *Melody, Dance,* and *Song.* We
have feen, that an Union of Narration
and concurrent Shouts of Praife takes
Place even in the rude Feftivals of the
favage Tribes : 'Tis altogether natural,
then, to fuppofe, when *Letters* had given Accents to the Rapture of the furrounding Audience, and moulded the
Ode into Form, that this Union which
Nature had eftablifhed, fhould be upheld. Though, therefore, the firft Rife
and Progrefs of the tragic Species in
GREECE were hid in Darknefs, through
a Want of recording Hiftory, yet, from
a Similarity of Caufes and Effects which
we find among the barbarous Nations
of AMERICA, we might fairly conclude,
that it had not a *cafual,* but a *certain*
Rife from *Nature ;* according to the Principles here given.

But ancient Hiftory is not filent on
this Subject. It gives us a Variety of
Facts, which overturn the common Syftem, and tend to confirm what is here
advanced. PLATO fays exprefly, that
" Tragedy

" Tragedy was very ancient in the City
" of ATHENS, and performed there, long
" before the Age of THESPIS [a]." We
are affured, on the Authority of other
Writers, that " a Report prevailed in
" GREECE, that certain tragic Poets
" had in ancient Times contended at the
" Tomb of THESEUS [b]." SUIDAS even
mentions EPIGENES by Name, *one* tragic Poet, out of *fifteen*, who were prior to
the Age of THESPIS.

But a ftill ftronger Evidence prefents
itfelf : For even the very *Subftance* and
Form of one of thefe rude Outlines of
favage Tragedy remains in feveral refpectable Authors of Antiquity : I mean, in
their Accounts of the Celebration of the

---

[a] MINOS.

[b] This is afferted by SCALIGER, in the cleareft
Terms ; and is alledged by him as a Proof of the
Exiftence of Tragedy, before the Age of THESPIS.
" Tragediam vero effe Rem antiquam conftat ex Hif-
" toria : ad THESEI namque Sepulchrum certaffe Tra-
" gicos legimus :" (De Poet. l. i. c. 5.) On what Authority He fays this, I know not. If any ancient Author hath afferted it, this Conteft muft have been held at
the Place where the Remains of THESEUS had been in-
terred before they were brought to ATHENS by CIMON ;
for that Event happened in the Time of SOPHOCLES.

Pythian

Pythian Games. Thefe were firft celebrated in the Times of APOLLO himfelf,
and contained a mimetic Narration, by
poetic Song, Melody, and *Dance,* of his Victory over the *Python.* This Reprefentation was called the *Pythian Nomos ;* and
underwent the following Changes or Improvements through feveral fucceffive Periods of Antiquity. " The Poem called
" *Nomos* had APOLLO for it's Subject;
" and took it's Name from *Him :* For
" APOLLO was ftiled *Nomimos,* becaufe
" in ancient Times, when the whole *Choir*
" ufed to fing the *Nomos* to the *Pipe* or
" *Lyre,* CHRYSOTHEMIS the *Cretan* was
" the firft who, clad in a fplendid Robe,
" and playing on the Harp, fung the
" Nomos *alone,* in *Imitation* of APOLLO's
" Victory ; and being much applauded,
" *this Form* of the Conteft *remained to*
" *After-Ages* [c]." What this *Form* was,
we

----

[c] Certamen apud Delphos antiquitus fuit Citharædo-
rum, Pæanem in Laudem Dei canentium. *Strabo* L. ix.
Nomos quidem in Apollinem *confcriptus ;* a quo Apel-
lationem fumpfit. Apollo enim *nomimos* appellatus eft,
quia *Veteribus Choros conftituentibus,* & ad Tibiam vel
Lyram *Nomen canentibus,* Chryfothemis Cretenfis primus
ftola

we learn from the following Accounts.
The Poem was divided into *five Parts*
or *Acts.* " The firſt contained the *Pre-*
"*paration* for the Fight; the ſecond, the
" Challenge; the third exhibited the Fight
" itſelf; the fourth, the *Victory* of APOL-
" LO; the fifth contained the *Triumph* of
" the God, who *danced* after his Victory
" [*d*]."—" It appears that TERPANDER
" improved the *Nomos,* by adding the *he-*
" *roic Meaſure:* After Him, ARION inlarg-
" ed it greatly; being both a *Poet* and
" a *Performer* on the *Harp.* PHRYNES
" introduced a *new Circumſtance;* for he
" joined the *Hexameter* with the *vari-*

ſtola uſus inſigni, & accepta Cithara, *Apollinem imitatus*
(the Original is ſtronger ; ως μιμησιν τυ Απολλωνος) *ſolus cecinit*
Nomon : qui cum valde probatus eſſet, permanſit hic
Modus Certaminis. *Proclus apud Photium. Bibl. Ed.*
Hoeſch. p. 982.

[*d*] Pythici vero nomi, qui Tibia canitur, partes
quinque ſunt ; Rudimentum, Provocatio, Iambicum,
Spondeum, Ovatio. Repreſentatio autem eſt Modus quidem Pugnæ Apollinis contra Draconem.—Et in ipſo Ex-
perimento Locum circumſpicit, num Pugnæ conveniens
ſit :—In Provocatione vero, provocat Draconem :—Sed
in Iambico pugnat :——Spondeum vero Dei Victoriam
repreſentat :—et in Ovatione, Deus ad victorialia Carmina
ſaltat.—*Jul. Pollux. Onom.* l. iv. c. 10.

" *ous*

" *ous. Meafure* [*e*]."—In a later Period,
this poetic and mufical Reprefentation was
" formally eftablifhed at DELPHI, after
" the *Criffæan* War [*f*]." Afterwards the
Amphictyons added a Conteft of *Mufic
merely inftrumental* [*g*]; but preferved what
had been practifed in former Times :
" There was the *Song* to the *Harp*, as
" *formerly;* there was the *Song* to the *Tibia*
" or *Pipe;* and there was the Pipe itfelf
" *without Song* [*h*]." This Addition of Mufic *merely inftrumental* was likewife *imitative;* being defigned as a *mimetic Defcription,* by *mere Melody,* of the Battle between
APOLLO and the *Python.* It confifted
likewife of five Parts, correfponding with

[*e*] Terpandrum vero Nomon abfolviffe apparet, cum
adhibuiffet heroicum Carmen : Poft, Arion Methymnæus
non parum auxit, Poeta ipfe & Citharædus. Phrynes vero
Mitylenæus novam Rationem commentus eft : Hexame-
trum enim cum foluto Carmine conjunxit. *Proclus apud
Photium :* ib.

[*f*] Inftitutum a Delphis *poft Criffæum Bellum.*

[*g*] Adjecerunt autem Citharædis Tibicines, et qui Cithara luderent *fine cantu,* modularenturque Carmen, quod
Nomos five Modus Pythius dicebatur.--*Strabo,* l. ix.

[*h*] Certamina inftituerunt Amphictyones ; Cantus ad
Citharam, ut pridem : Cantus item ad Tibiam ; ipfarum
etiam per fe Tibiarum.--*Paufanias; in Phocicis.*

thofe

thofe of the ancient Song [*i*].—" Timos-
" thenes, in the Time of the fecond
" *Ptolemy*, writ a Poem defcriptive and
" explanatory of this mufical Contention :
" According to this Author, the Subject
" was the Victory of Apollo over the
" Serpent. The firft Part was the Prelude
" to Battle ; the fecond was the Beginning
" of the Engagement ; the third was the
" Battle itfelf ; the fourth was the Pæan
" or Triumph on the Victory ; the fifth
" was an Imitation of the Agonies and Hif-
" fing of the dying Serpent [*k*]."

Now, though thefe ancient Authors differ
from each other in two or three trifling
Circumftances ; yet, as to every thing *effential*, they *perfectly agree*. And from
their

[*i*] Quinque funt ejus Partes ; anacrufis, ampcira, ka-
takeleufmos, Iambi & Dactyli, fyringes feu Fiftulæ fibilæ.
Strabo. ib.

[*k*] Carmen compofuit Timofthenes fecundi Ptolemæi
Claffi Præfectus :—Vult autum Apollinis adverfus Draconem Certamen celebrari eo Carmine : & anacrufin fignifi-
care Præludium ; ampeiran Certaminis Initium ; katake-
leufmon ipfam Pugnam ; Iambum & Dactylum Pæanem
qui Victoriæ acciniter, talibus Modis, five Rythmis, quo-
rum Hymnus quidem proprius eft ; Iambus autem *(defunt
quædam)* & iambizare ; Fiftulas autem Mortem imitatas
Serpentis,

their concurrent Evidence, we have clear Proof of the following Facts. 1. That the immediate Followers of APOLLO began thefe *poetic* and *mufical* Contefts. 2. That till CHRYSOTHEMIS appeared (in, or near the Time of APOLLO) there fubfifted only a *Choir*. 3. That *He* firft fung the *Epifode*, fingle and alone. 4. That his Song was a *mimetic Narration*, or *Imitation* of APOLLO's Victory. 5. That the *Form* which He gave to This, *continued* through fucceeding Times. 6. That this Poem was divided into *five Parts* or *Acts*, containing a *progreſſive Defcription* and *Imitation* of the Battle and Victory. And laftly, that *Songs of Triumph, Exultation, Sarcafm,* and *Contempt,* together with a *correfpondent Dance,* accompanied the *narrative Epifode.* [*l*].

Thus,

Serpentis, Vitam cum Sibilis quibufdam finientis. *Strabo.* ib.—Thefe Paſſages are given in the Latin Tranſlations (which, though not always elegant, are fufficiently correct) that a greater Number of Readers may be inabled to judge of the Evidence.

[*l*] SCALIGER is of Opinion, that the *Dance* was *mimetic* of the *whole Narration* or *Action*, and divided into the fame Number of *Acts*. " At vero feorfum Saltatio " *haud illi abfimilis* edebatur, in *totidem Actus* æque diftri- " buta."

Thus, in this moſt ancient *Pythian Song*, as delivered down from the Times of A-POLLO himſelf, and performed and augmented through the ſucceeding Periods of ancient GREECE, we have the very *Subſtance* and *Form* of a firſt rude Eſſay towards Tragedy, divided into *five Acts*, and compounded of *poetic Narration*, *imitative Muſic*, *Dance*, and *Choral Song*. —And it is worthy of ſingular Obſervation, that through this whole repreſentative Scene, of APOLLO *ſinging, dancing*, and *praiſing his own Exploits;* the ancient *Greek Hiſtorians* tranſport us, as it were, into the Wilds of *modern America;* and preſent to us the *genuine Picture* of a *ſavage Chieftain* [m].

It appears, therefore, that Tragedy had a much earlier and deeper Foundation in ancient GREECE, than the accidental Adventure of THESPIS and his Route: That

" buta." Poet. l. i. c. 23. If indeed this was added, it amounts to a ſtrict *dramatic Repreſentation*. For, as the ſame learned Critic ſays elſewhere, " Sane Ludi ſunt ta- " citæ Fabulæ; Fabulæ vero Ludi loquentes." ib. c. xxii. But as this Circumſtance is not ſo clearly delivered as the reſt, I lay no Streſs on it.

[m] See the Deſcription of the ſavage Song Feaſt, from LAFITAU. Sect. ii.

it

it arofe from *Nature*, and an unforced *Union* and *Progreſſion* of *Melody*, *Dance*, and poetic *Song*.

At the fame Time it is manifeſt, that THESPIS added *ſomething* to the rude and ſavage Form of Tragedy, as it exiſted in *his* Age. 'Tis probable that He was the *firſt Declaimer* or *Interlocutor* to *his own Choir*; nay, perhaps, was the firſt in ancient GREECE who compleatly changed the *narrative Epiſode* into the *dramatic Form*; that he firſt eſtabliſhed the *Profeſſion* of a *Player* in ATTICA, and firſt tranſ-ported his *Company* from one Village to another ; whereas, before his Time, the Exhibitions of the rude tragic Scene had been fixed, and merely *incidental* [*n*]. This Inſtitution of an itinerant Company muſt neceſſarily increaſe the general Attention of ATTICA to theſe rude tragic Scenes: the Change of the *narrative* into the *dra-matic Form* might naturally induce SOLON to tax THESPIS with being a *Liar* (ὑποκριτης): And hence the Opinion ſeems firſt to have ariſen, that THESPIS was the *Inventor* of this Species [*o*].

18. " In

[*n*] HOR. *Ep. ad* PIS.—DIOG. LAERT. SOLON.

[*o*] The

18. " In Procefs of Time, this barba-
" rous Scene improved into a more per-
" fect Form : Inftead of *relating*, they *re-*
" *prefented* by an *affumed Character*, and
" by *Action* and *Song*, ,thofe great or terri-
" ble Atchievements which their Heroes
" had performed." How foon the favage
Tribes fall into this Kind of dramatic
Reprefentation, we have already feen [*p*]:

[*o*] The moft learned BENTLEY fell into the common Syftem, with Regard to the Rife of Tragedy:
Attempting to prove, that THESPIS was its *Inventor.*
Thus, for Want of the true *Data*, and from an Unac-
quaintance with Man in his favage State, this great Critic
hath thrown out a Chain of Errors : While, if he had
been led up to the true Fountains of Information, he
would probably have caught the various Progreffions of
Poetry at a Glance.

Mr. BOYLE, in his Examination of BENTLEY's Differtation, feems once or twice to get out of the common Track of Criticifm on this Subject : Yet, for Want
of knowing the true Origin of Tragedy, as founded in
human Nature, he throws little or no Light upon the
Queftion. He infifts, that Tragedy is more ancient than
THESPIS, on the Authority of PLATO and LAERTIUS :
But he falls again into the vulgar Track, in affirming,
that till the Time of THESPIS, the *Epifode* had no Exiftence, but only the *Choir*. In Confutation of which
Opinion we have now fhewn, that the full Form of favage
Tragedy had appeared many Ages before, in the ancient Celebration of the *Pythian Games.*

[*p*] Above, Sect. ii.

How

How natural fuch a Progreffion of Art
muft be to the human Mind, will appear
by reflecting, that dramatic *Action* is but
another Mode of *Narration ;* and that
even the *Narration* of the favage Tribes
is found to have fuch a Mixture of *Action* in it, as ftrongly tends to produce
the dramatic Imitation [*q*]. Time, therefore, and repeated Efforts muft naturally
advance the *narrative Epifode* into *perfonal
Reprefentation.* And thus we are arrived
at the Form which Tragedy wore at
Athens, when the inventive Genius of
Eschylus advanced the Art one Step
higher ; and by adding a *fecond Perfon* to
the Drama, brought in the Ufe of *Dialogue.*

Here, for the Sake of Truth, we muft
again depart from the general Body of
Critics ; moft of whom, from Aristotle
down to our own Times, unite in fuppofing that Eschylus was only a cafual
Imitator of Homer, and drew the Idea
of all his Tragedies from the Iliad. A
noble Critic of our own Country hath
affirmed this in the feweft and ftrongeft
Terms ; and fays, that " There was no

[*q*] Above, Sect. ii.

" more

" more left for Tragedy to do after him
" (HOMER) than to erect a Stage, and
" draw his Dialogues and Characters into
" Scenes [r]."

It may be deemed prefumptuous, perhaps, to queftion a Point wherein the great
Mafter-Critic of GREECE hath himfelf
decided.   But let us remember, that the
Days are now paft, when it was held a
Point of Honour, to *fwear* to the *Opinions*
of a *Mafter*.   ARISTOTLE is often admirable, generally judicious, yet fometimes
perhaps miftaken, even in his Judgment
of Men and Things relative to his own
Country.   He was more efpecially capa-
ble of being mifled by the common Opinion in this Point ; in which neither He
nor any of his Countrymen could be fufficiently informed, for Want of a competent Knowledge of the Genius and
Character of favage Manners.

That ESCHYLUS was not a mere Imitator of HOMER, that he was a great and
original Poet, who exalted his Art one
Degree beyond his Predeceffors in his own
Country, feems a Point which collateral

[r] *Characteriftics*, vol. i. p. 197.

Argu-

Arguments ftrongly confirm. We are informed, in general Terms, that there were
no lefs than fixteen tragic Poets who writ.
before him: And the Probability is much
ftronger, that he fhould draw his Improvement from the *fcenic* Reprefentations
already eftablifhed, in which he found
one dramatic Perfon and an accompanying *Choir*, which incidentally ftood in
the Place of a fecond Perfon, and often
fuftained a Kind of Dialogue with the
principal Interlocutor [s]; than that he
fhould have Recourfe to HOMER's Poems,
in which no dramatic Reprefentation was
to be found.

To this Argument may be added another, drawn from the Style and Manner
of ESCHYLUS, fo different from that of
HOMER. For HOMER is equal, large,
flowing, and harmonious: ESCHYLUS is
uneven, concife, abrupt, and rugged:
The one leads you through the grand

[s] This Opinion receives a ftrong Confirmation
from the following Circumftance, that in the *Greek Tragedies* which have come down to us, whenever there is a
fingle Interlocutor on the Stage, the *Choir* frequently maintains a *Dialogue* with him.—Concerning the *original* Nature of the *Choir*, fee below Art. xix. Note.

but

but gentle Declivities of Hill and Dale;
the other carries you over a continued
Chain of Rocks and Precipices. Now if
HOMER had been the Model of ESCHY-
LUS, fome *Similarity* of *Manner* would
probably have enfued.

A third and ftill ftronger Proof arifes
from the effential Difference of their Subjects, both in Extent and Nature: In Extent, becaufe the one is of *long*, the other
of *fhort* Duration: In Nature, becaufe
HOMER's Poems are chiefly employed in
the Exhibition of *Character* and *Manners*;
thofe of ESCHYLUS in the Reprefentation
of *Terror* and *Diftrefs*. Had he been that
mere Imitator of HOMER which the Critics have adjudged him, and had nothing
to do but to erect a Stage, and to draw
HOMER's Dialogues into Scenes, he would
have been content to have taken his Subjects from the *Iliad*, and, according to
HORACE's fober Rule, have never ventured beyond the Siege of *Troy* [*t*]. He
would have brought upon the Stage the
Anger of ACHILLES, the Battle of PARIS
and MENELAUS, the Parting of HECTOR

[*t*] RECTIUS ILIACOS, &c.

I   and

and ANDROMACHE, the Feats of DIO-
MEDE ; and would have contrafted the
Strength of AJAX with the Cunning of
ULYSSES. Nothing of all this appears:
On the contrary, his *Subjects* and *Manner*
are equally *his own ;* and *both* of a Ge-
nius oppofite to thofe of HOMER [*u*].

What PLUTARCH fays of HOMER,
though brought for the contrary Purpofe,
tends to confirm all that is here ad
vanced. " Even Tragedy took its Rife
" from HOMER : For his Poems com-
" prehend every thing that is *fublime*
" and *great* [*w*]." This, you will fay, is
a very infufficient Reafon, becaufe the
Critic forgets the *pathetic* and the *terri-*

[*u*] It is faid, indeed, of ESCHYLUS, that he called
his Tragedies no more than " Fragments of the magni-
" ficent Entertainment given by HOMER." Now this Expreffion being only *metaphorical*, we ought to interpret it in
that Senfe only, to which a Comparifon of their Writings
leads us. And, as it appears that there is no Refemblance
between them, either in the *particular Subjects,* or in the
Manner of treating them; the only rational Interpretation
that can be given, feems to be this ; " that the Subjects
" of his Tragedies were only fmall *Morfels* or *Fragments*
" of the *Grecian Story ;* whereas HOMER had given a
" *general Syftem* of their fabulous Hiftory, both in a more
" *extenfive* and a more *connected* Manner.
    [*w*] *In Vita* HOMERI.

ble,

ble, which were the effential Conftituents
of the Greek Tragedy.   But mark the
Sequel; which is ftill more extraordinary.
" Neither do they (Homer's Poems) con-
" tain Defcriptions of thofe *atrocious Ac-*
" *tions* which have been feigned by the
" later Tragedians, fuch as *Inceft*, and the
" *Murder* of *Parents* or *Children*.   Nay,
" whenever he happens to touch on any
" thing of this Kind, he always *foftens*
" and throws it *into Shades* [*x*]."   Thus
while Plutarch is labouring to prove,
that the *Greek* Tragedy was *drawn* from
Homer, he proves, that Homer's Poems
were *deftitute* of that which was of the
Effence of the *Greek* Tragedy.

Scaliger is a venerable Exception to
the general Body of the Critics on this
Subject ; and feems to have viewed the
Queftion in its true Light. " In the *Iliad*
" (faith he) there is nothing like the *Pro-*
" *greffion* of a *Tragedy*, if you take the
" *whole* together : For, from Beginning
" to End, there is a *perpetual* Succeffion
" of *Deaths :* He begins with a Peftilence,
" which deftroys more Men than the

[*x*] *In Vita* Homeri.

I 2   " whole

" whole War [*y*]." The Critic then goes
on to prove, by a large Enumeration of
Circumftances, the *Iliad* hath very few of
the effential Characteriftics of *Tragedy*.

We may fairly conclude, then, that
the Improvement which Tragedy received
from ESCHYLUS was not *cafual*, but the
Refult of a *natural Progreffion :* That he
drew not from HOMER's Poems, as a
mere Imitator ; but exalted his Art one
Step higher, from the Force of true *Genius*
in the *tragic* Species.

What followed is well known : SOPHO-
CLES added a *third* Perfon to the Drama:
And by this Improvement is faid by the
Critics to have *compleated* the Form of
Tragedy. The Truth of their Decifion I
much doubt : But this Difquifition lies
beyond the Limits of our prefent Enquiry.

19. " As the Choir was eftablifhed by
" Nature and Cuftom, and animated their
" Solemnities by *Dance* as well as *Song;*
" the Melody, Dance, and Song, did of
" Courfe regulate each other ; and the
" Ode or Song naturally fell into *Stanzas*
" of fome *particular* Kind." This arofe
by an eafy Progreffion from the favage

[*y*] *Poët.* l. i. c. 5.

State ;

State; where " they who dance, go round
" in a circular Movement, and after a
" fhort Interval begin a fecond [z]." The
Greeks not only fell into this Manner, but
improved upon it: They went round, firft
to the one Hand, then to the other, and
then paufed. The Learned have found
out myftical Reafons for thefe circular
Movements; referring them to the Motion of the Planets [a]. Much Labour
cannot be neceffary for the Confutation
of thefe Refinements, as the Practice arofe
fo evidently from the Dictates of Nature;
It was a natural and fenfible Improvement; for the plain Reafon of *preventing*
Giddinefs, which arifeth from running
round in the fame Circle.

Let us attend, therefore, to its Confequences. As each *Dance* or *Return* was
marked by it's peculiar *Meafure,* this of
Courfe fixed both the *Melody* and poetic
Numbers of the accompanying Song: And
as they likewife fung during the *Interval*
of *Reft,* we fee, that from this eafy Improvement on the favage Song-Feaft, the

[z] See Sect. ii. [a] ATHENÆUS *Deip.* l. i.

I 3   *Strophe,*

Strophe, Antiſtrophe, and *Epode,* naturally
aroſe [*b*].

20. Ano-

[*b*] By thus trácing the tragic *Choir* to it's true
Foundation, the *ſavage Song-Feaſt;* we are now inabled
to give a clear and eaſy Solution to a Difficulty which
hath embarraſſed all the Critics. It hath been held a
Circumſtance unaccountable or abſurd, that the *Choir,* in
ſeveral of the ancient *Greek Tragedies,* ſhould be made *privy*
to ſome of the moſt *atrocious Deſigns,* and yet ſhould not
reveal them, though it's *Character* was confeſſedly *moral.*
This indeed, on the common Suppoſition, that the
Choir originally made an eſſential Part of the *dramatic
Perſons,* is a thorough Abſurdity. But in Reality it appears in the *ſavage Song-Feaſt,* that they who *recite* or
repreſent the *Action,* are a *Body* quite diſtinct from the *Choir;*
and that the *Choir,* in it's *original* State, is indeed the *Audience* who ſurround the *Narrator* or *Actor,* and *anſwer* him
at every *Pauſe,* with Shouts of *Triumph, Approbation,* or
Diſlike. This being ſo, how could they (the *Choir* or
Audience) properly *reveal* any ſecret Deſigns, either good
or bad ?—To whom ſhould they *reveal* them ? To each
other ?—This was needleſs, becauſe they knew them already.—Muſt they, then, reveal them to the *Actors* of
the Drama ? This could only have confounded the Repreſentation, and deſtroyed the Plot. It would have
been preciſely on a Level with the Practice of an honeſt
Country Lad, who was preſent at the Repreſentation of
Othello : When he foreſaw, that Iago's Treachery
was likely to end tragically for poor Desdemona, he
called aloud to Othello, " *Sir, the Raſcal lies : he ſtole
" the Handkerchief himſelf.*"—This naturally leads to the
Elucidation of another Circumſtance. In the Beginning of
the

20. " Another Confequence of the ef-
" tablifhed *Choir* was a ftrict and unva-
" ried Adherence to the *Unities* of *Place*
" and *Time."* This Effect is fo manifeft
as to need little Illuftration.   A nu-
I 4   merous

the Time of Eschylus, the *Choir* confifted of no lefs than
fifty Perfons: Afterwards the Number was leffened to *fifteen.*
How came it to pafs, that in the more barbarous Periods
the Number fhould be fo much greater ? Manifeftly (on
the Principles here given) becaufe *that* rude Age bordered
on the *favage* Times, when the *whole Audience* had *fym-
pathized* with the *narrative Actor*, and became as *one general Choir.*

This Solution naturally clears up another Circumftance,
which is unaccountable on the common Syftem.   If the
Choir were *originally* a Part of the *dramatic Actors*, why
were they placed in a *Balcony* or *Gallery, feparate fr\m the
Stage ?* No good Reafon can be affigned.   But if we fup-
pofe them to have been *originally* the *Spectators* of the
Drama, we fee they were in their *natural* and *proper
Situation.*

But to this it may be objected, " that the *Choir* fometimes
" maintains a *Dialogue* with the *Actor,* in the *Greek* Tra-
" gedies ; and ought therefore to be regarded as a *dra-
" matic Perfon.*"—To this (which hath been obferved
above) it is reply'd, that though the *Choir* fometimes
fpeaks, yet this is only by it's *Leader,* and then only *occafionally,* and from *Neceffity,* to fill the *Place* of *another
Actor,* when no more than one or two are upon the Stage.
For this Reafon Eschylus ufes the Expedient .oftener
than his Succeffors, becaufe his dramatic Perfons were
fewer.   But though the *Choir* fometimes fpeak by their
Leader,

merous *Choir*, maintaining their Station
through the whole Performance, gave fo
forcible a Conviction to the Senfes, of
the *Samenefs* of *Place*, and the *Shortnefs*
of *Time*, that any Deviation from this
apparent Unity muft have fhocked the
Imagination with an Improbability too
grofs to be indured. Notwithftanding all
the Panegyrics of the Critics, therefore,
upon the Greek Tragedians on Account
of thefe *Unities;* it is evident, they arofe
in the rudeft Periods ; and were continued
through the more polifhed Ages, on the

Leader, yet they never take Part in the *Action ;* as fufficiently appears by their not revealing the Secrets of it.

It may be urged again, that in the *Eumenides* and *Iketides*
of ESCHYLUS, the *Choir* is certainly to be confidered as
a *dramatic Perfon*, becaufe they are indeed the *chief Actors* in the Drama.   True ; they are fo: but though this
Objection looks formidable, yet on a deeper Confideration, the Bugbear will vanifh.—ESCHYLUS was defirous
to reprefent an Action of *fifty Furies*, and another of *fifty
Danaids*, at a Time when only *two dramatic Perfons* were
allowed by Cuftom to come on the Stage together.   What
Expedient could he ufe ?   Why, furely, no other than
That which we find he *hath* ufed : To throw thefe *numerous Bodies* into the Form of a Choir ; and thus he gained
them Admittance on the Stage.—To fpeak with Preci-
fion, therefore, we ought to fay, that the Action of thefe
two Tragedies paffeth *without a Choir*, that is, without
any fuppofed *Spectators* who *take no Part in it.*

fame

fame Principle of untaught Nature and
eftablifhed Cuftom.

21. " Not only the Part of the tragic
" *Choir*, but the *Epifode*, or *interlocutory*
" Part was alfo *Sung*." The moft fenfible
of the Critics have ever regarded this as
a Circumftance equally unnatural and unaccountable. Thus DACIER fpeaks. " It
" muft be owned, that we cannot well
" comprehend, how Mufic *(Melody)* could
" ever be confidered as in any Refpect
" making a Part of Tragedy : For if there
" be any thing in the World that is at Va-
" riance with *tragic Action*, it is *Song* [*c*]."
The learned Critic is fo fhocked with this
fuppofed Union, in Appearance fo unnatural, that upon the whole he queftions
its Exiftence ; and is of Opinion, that
when ARISTOTLE fpeaks of *Mufic*, as
being annexed to *Tragedy*, he fpeaks of
the *Choir* only [*d*]. This, however, is
contrary to the united Voice of Antiquity,
which univerfally admits the Fact, though
its Origin was never accounted for. But
how naturally this Union took Place in
ancient Tragedy, we now clearly difco-

[*c*] *Sur* ARISTOTE, p. 85, &c.   [*d*] Ibid.

ver,

ver, by inveftigating the Rife and Progrefs of this Poem from the favage State.
For it appears, that the Epic and *Ode*
were both fung from the earlieft Periods;
and therefore, when they became *united*,
and by that Union formed the tragic
Species, they of Courfe maintained the
•fame Appendage of *Melody*, which Nature
and Cuftom had already given them.

The *Abbé du* Bos endeavours to prove,
indeed, that the *Song* which was employed
in the *Epifode* of ancient Tragedy was no
more than a Kind of *regulated* or *meafured Declamation* [e]. But his Inquiries
are partial; for he goes no higher than
to the Practice of the *Romans :* And it is
probable, from feveral Circumftances, that
in the late Period when the *Romans* borrowed their Mufic from the *Greeks*, the
Tragic *Song* had been brought down from
a *meafured Melody* to a Kind of *regulated
Declamation*. Thus Tully mentions the
Cantus Subobfcurus; and again faith, " De-
" licatiores funt falfæ Voculæ quam certæ
" et feveræ." But though thefe, with feveral other Arguments alledged by the
Abbé, feem to imply that the tragic *Song*

[e] *Reflec. Crit.* Part iii. ç. 4, &c.

was

was little more than a meafured Recitation ; yet this will by no Means prove, that
a more full and direct Song had not been
ufed in Tragedy through the more early
Periods.   In the Courfe of this Differtation, the Practice of *finging* Tragedy hath
been traced from its firft Rife in favage
Manners ; which at once deftroys the *Improbability* of the Cuftom, and proves that
it was even founded in Nature ; a Circumftance, of which the *Abbé* had not the
leaft Sufpicion.   This Foundation being
laid, we cannot but liften attentively to
what the Writers of GREECE tell us on
this Subject : Now thefe unite in inform-
ing us, that the *Epifode* of Tragedy was
Sung ; and even name the *Modes* of Mufic which were appropriated to the *Epifode* in Contradiftinction to the *Choir* [*f*].
That the *Song* fhould approach nearer, by
Degrees, to mere Declamation, will appear probable, when we confider the gradual Separations which fucceffively took
Place in the mufical Art, during the fucceffive Periods of GREECE and ROME.
To mention only one Inftance here, fimilar to what we now treat of : ARISTO-

[*f*] ARISTOT. *Prob.* 19.

TLE

TLE informs as, that in *His* Time the *Rhapfodifts*, whofe Profeffion it was to *fing* the Poems of HOMER and HESIOD, were beginning to make Inroads into the ancient Practice ; and now *recited* thofe *Poems*, which in *former Times* had been always *fung* [g].

The *Abbé* falls into an Error with Réfpect to the *Dance*, parallel to that which he adopts with Regard to the *Melody* of the Ancients. As he infifts that their *tragic Melody* was only a *meafured Recitation*, fo he affirms, that their *tragic Dance* was no more than *Action* [h]. It is true, that in the later Periods of *Rome*, when the mufical Separations had taken Place, this was the general Meaning of the Word *Saltatio :* And hence, as in his Opinion of the tragic Song, his Miftake arofe. For it is evident from the concurrent Teftimony of the elder *Greek* Writers, that the *tragic Dance* was performed in the very Manner here defcribed. We now fee, that this *Dance* (no lefs than the *tragic Song*) arofe from untaught Nature; and that it was the genuine Parent of the *Strophe*, *Antiftrophe*, and *Epode*.

[g] *Poët.* c. 26.　[h] *Reflec.* Part iii. c. 13.

22. ‘ As

22. " As the *Greek* Nation was of a
" *fierce* and *warlike* Character, their tragic
" Reprefentations rowled chiefly on Sub-
" jects of *Diftrefs* and *Terror*."—On this
Topic, I doubt whether ARISTOTLE hath
not miftaken an *Effect* for a *Caufe*. For
he fays, that " Tragedy, by Means of
" *Pity* and *Terror*, purgeth in us *Thofe* and
" other fuch like *Paffions* [*i*]." MARCUS
AURELIUS [*k*], MILTON [*l*], DACIER
[*m*], and BRUMOY [*n*], all underftand him,
as meaning that Tragedy was formed
with this View.   It is not the Writer's
Defign to remark on this great Critic, farther than what relates to his main Subject.   Therefore it will fuffice to fay, that
if ARISTOTLE meant to affign this *moral
End*, as the *Caufe* why Tragedy affumed
this Form in ancient GREECE, and a-
dopted Subjects of *Diftrefs* and *Terror*,
He feems to have taken That for a *Caufe*,
which was a *natural Effect* of the ruling
Manners of the *Greek* Republics.   The Reafons which fupport the general Truth, already given in the correfpondent Arti-

[*i*] *Poët.* c. 6.   [*k*] L. xi. Art. 6.   [*l*] *Preface to*
SAMSON AGONISTES.   [*m*] *Poët. d'Arift.*   [*n*] *Theat.
des Grecs*, tom. i. p. 85.

cle,

cle, will hold their Force when applied
here.   For thus the *Greeks* animated each
other to *Victory* and *Revenge*, by a Reprefentation of what their Friends had *done*
and *fuffered*.   Thefe Subjects would likewife be moft accommodated to the natural
Tafte of the poetic Chiefs of fuch a People ; whofe *Atchievements* produced and
abounded with Events of *Diftrefs* and
Terror.   Such then was the natural Origin and Adoption of thefe Subjects, in the
Greek Tragedy : But after they were eftablifhed on this Foundation, 'tis probable
that the Statefmen encouraged and applied
them to the *Ends* of Policy.   For as the
leading View of a fierce and warlike People
muft be to *deftroy Pity* and *Fear ;* fo
This would moft effectually be done, by
making themfelves familiar with diftrefsful and terrible Reprefentations.   Under
thefe Reftrictions the Opinion of Aristotle may have a Foundation in Nature : Farther than this ; and as applied
to any People whofe End is not *War* and
Conqueft, it carries the Appearance of a
refined Idea, which hath no Foundation
in Nature.   The grand fcenic Reprefentations of the *Peruvians* and *Chinefe* (as
                                                        will

will appear below [o]) whofe leading Object was *Peace*, are known to be of a
quite contrary Nature, formed on their
gentler Manners : and fuch as would have
been altogether incompatible with the ferocious Character, and infipid to the Tafte
of the Tribes of ancient Greece.

23. " Their Tragedy being defigned as
" a vifible Reprefentation of their ancient
" Gods and Heroes, they invented a Me-
" thod of ftrengthening the Voice, and
" aggrandizing the Vifage and Perfon, as
" the Means of compleating the Refem-
" blance." It is generally known, that
the old *Grecian Gods* were fuppofed to be
of a Stature *exceeding* that of *ordinary*
Men : The true Reafon of that Opinion
was, becaufe in the early Ages they (like
every other barbarous People [p]) felected
the *talleft* and *ftrongeft* Men for their
Chiefs : Which Chiefs in Courfe of Time
became their *Gods.* Hence the *Bufkin* and
Mafque had their natural Birth : For the
firft *hightened* the *Stature*, as the fecond *inlarged* the *Vifage*, and *ftrengthened* the *Voice*
of the dramatic Actor. And although the

[o] Sect. viii.
[p] See Lafitau, and other Travellers.

common

common Accounts mention nothing of the *Inlargement* of the *Body* ; yet we learn from LUCIAN, that the *Breaſt*, *Back*, and all the *Limbs*, were *amplified* in Proportion to the *Viſage* and *Stature* [q] : Manifeſtly as the Means of compleating the Reſemblance of their Gods and Heroes.

By thus tracing the *Buſkin* and *Maſque* to their true Origin, we ſhall now be able to give a Reaſon for a Fact, which hath hitherto been regarded as merely the Effect of Whim and Caprice. THESPIS and his *Company* bedaubed their Faces with the *Lees* of *Wine*. Whence aroſe this Practice, ſeemingly ſo wild? THESPIS and his *Company* were the Votaries of BACCHUS, and exhibited his Exploits, and ſung his Praiſes to their Countrymen : Their Uſe of the *Lees* of *Wine*, therefore, was intended as the Means of compleating the *Reſemblance* of their *drunken God* and his *Crew*.

24. " As their *tragic Poets* were *Singers*, " ſo they were *Actors*, and generally per- " formed ſome capital Part, in their own " Pieces for the Stage." This Fact hath generally been held extraordinary and un-

[q] *De Saltatione.*

ac-

accountable : And hath been resolved, it
seems, by some Talkers on this Subject,
into the *Want* of *Actors* in the *early* Periods. We now clearly discover a contrary Cause : The Practice took Place when
the *highest* Characters were *proud* to sig-
nalize themselves as *Actors :* When Legiflators and Bards assumed the *Lyrist's* and
Actor's Character, as the Means of civilizing their furrounding Tribe : Therefore, till some extraordinary Change in
Manners and Principles should ensue, the
original Union established by Nature and
Custom was of Course maintained in
Greece. Sophocles was the first on
Record who quitted this honourable Em-
ploy : And He, only because his Voice
was unequal to the Vastness of the *Athenian* Stage. That he quitted it on this
Principle alone, appears from his Conduct
on other Occasions: For he not only *Sung*
his *own* Verses, but likewise *led* the *Dance*
at a public Triumph [r].

25. " Musical *Contests*, consisting of
" *Melody* and *poetic Song*, were admitted
" as public Exercises in the *Grecian* States."

[r] Athen. *Deipn.* l. i.

K   For

For the Truth of This, we have the con-current Evidence of many ancient Writers. That Union of *Gymnaftic* and *mufical* Ex-ercifes which took Place in the early Pe-riods of the *Greek* Republics, hath by fome Writers been regarded as *unnatural :* by all, as *accidental.* Thus a learned Au-thor fays, " To thefe *Gymnaftic* Exercifes " were added others of a quite *different* " *Nature* [*s*]." But by following this Ef-tablifhment up to it's firft Principles, we have now found, that in Faft the *Gym-naftic* Exercifes were originally a *Part* of the *mufical* [*t*], being no more than the improved *Dance,* which was a Branch of ancient *Mufic.* In Procefs of Time, as hath been proved, the *Dance* or *Gymnaftic* Art was generally feparated from the *Poem* and *Melody* : But it is remarkable, that in all their public Games or Contefts, from the earlieft to the lateft Periods, thefe feveral Branches of Mufic, either feparate or in Union, compofed the effen-tial Parts of their public Exhibitions.

The learned STRABO, PAUSANIAS, PRO-CLUS, and JULIUS POLLUX, have left us

[*s*] POTTER *Arch. Græc.* [*t*] See above, Art. xvii.

the

the moſt particular Account of the Riſe and Progreſs of the Pythian Games ; which entirely coincides with the Principles here given [*u*]. From the ancient Celebration of theſe, down to the Time when they were eſtabliſhed at DELPHI after the *Criſſæan* War, we ſee, the muſical Conteſt maintained it's original Savage Form, without any Separation of the Dance. " Afterwards the *Amphictyons,* under Eu-" RYLOCHUS, inſtituted the *equeſtrian* " and *gymnaſtic* Conteſt ; appointing a " Crown as the Conqueror's Reward [*w*]." Here, we find, in a later Period, the Eſtabliſhment aſſumed it's political Form ; a Separation enſued ; the *Dance* was heightened into the *Gymnaſtic* Art, for the Reaſons·aſſigned above.

We have already ſeen the Form of this muſical Conteſt, as deſcribed by STRABO and others [*x*]. We have obſerved, that they clearly deduce it's Origin from the Times of APOLLO himſelf [*y*]. SCALIGER, ſpeaking of the Riſe of theſe *Pythian* Games, makes no Doubt of their having been inſtituted by

[*u*] See above, Art. xvii.   [*w*] STRABO, l. ix.
[*x*] Art. xvii.   [*y*] Ibid.

APOLLO [z]. But not knowing the true Origin of the *Gymnaſtic* Art, as having originally made a Part of the *muſical*, and ſuppoſing (according to the common Syſtem) that theſe Games were eſtabliſhed as a mere *imitative Memorial* of the *particular Aſtion* performed, he adds with great Candour, " I wonder, conſidering that he " killed the *Python* with an *Arrow*, that " he did not inſtitute a *Contention* of *Ar-* " *chers*, rather than *Muſicians* [a]." This Doubt, ſo candidly expreſſed, throws new Light upon the Queſtion; and is a collateral Circumſtance of Proof, that theſe Games had their Origin in the ſavage *Song-Feaſt*, which in aftertimes branched out into the *Gymnaſtic* Arts.

So much concerning the Riſe and Progreſs of the *Pythian* Games; which ſufficiently clears our Subjeſt. As to the Origin and Progreſs of the Olympic Games, it is much hid in the Darkneſs of diſtant Ages. They are generally aſcribed to the *Idæan* HERCULES, who is ſaid to have given them the Name of *Olympic*. But if we attend to Arguments of Pro-

[z] *Poet.* l. i. c. 23.　　[a] Ibid.

bability,

bability, arifing from the Analogy of
Names, we fhall rather be led to at-
tribute their Inftitution to the *Olympian*
JUPITER; efpecially, as Tradition fup-
ports this Conjecture at leaft as ftrongly
as the other. For PAUSANIAS informs
us, that " there are who fay, that JU-
" PITER contended for Empire with SA-
" TURN, in this very Place: Others af-
" firm, that having vanquifhed the *Titans*,
" He (JUPITER) inftituted thefe Games, in
" which others too are faid to have been
" Conquerors; that APOLLO vanquifhed
" MERCURY in the *Race*, and overcame
" MARS at *boxing* [*b*]." All this agrees
fo entirely with the *Character* and *Contentions* of *favage Chieftains*, as to create
a ftrong Probability of the Truth of the
Tradition. This we know, however, that
Mufical Contefts made an effential Part of
thefe magnificent Exhibitions; and that
PINDAR fung his Odes, and was often
crowned as *Victor* in thefe public Contefts.

The *Ifthmian* and *Nemean* Games, having been inftituted in later Periods, when
a Separation of the Dance had been al-

[*b*] PAUSANIAS, l. v.

K 3   ready

ready made, and confequently the *Gym-naftic* Arts already eftablifhed, we cannot properly draw any Conclufions from Thefe, relative to the prefent Queftion.

The *tragic Contefts*, which followed on the Improvement of that Species of Poe-try, are too well known to need any par-ticular Delineation. Let it fuffice, that we have traced them up to their firft rude Form and Origin in the *mufical Conteft* at DELPHI, as defcribed by ancient Authors [*c*]. They were re-eftablifhed in their more improved State by CIMON, when that General brought the Remains of THE-SEUS to ATHENS. The three great tra-gic Bards, ESCHYLUS, SOPHOCLES, and EURIPIDES, all *contended*, and were *crown-ed* by Turns.

This general Eftablifhment of *mufical Contefts*, which hath been fo often held trifling and unaccountable, appears now to have been founded in true Policy and Wifdom. " For as the leading Articles " of their Religion, Morals, and Polity, " made a Part of their public Songs; fo, " public Contefts of this Kind were juftly " regarded as the fureft Means of keeping

[*c*] See above, Art. xvii.

" up

" up an Emulation of a moſt uſeful Na-
" ture; and of ſtrengthening the State, by
" inforcing the fundamental Principles of
" Society, in the moſt agreeable, moſt
" ſtriking, and moſt effectual Manner."

26. " The Profeſſion of *Bard* was held
" as very *honourable*, and of high Eſteem."
We have ſeen the Foundation of This, in
the thirteenth Article of the preſent Section.
For he was veſted with a Kind of public
Character; and if not an original Legiſlator, was at leaſt a ſubordinate and uſeful
Servant of the State: And as the Utility
of his Profeſſion was ſuch as aroſe from
Genius, perſonal Reſpect and Honour was
the natural Conſequence in a *well ordered*
Republic. The Facts which ſupport this
Truth, with regard to ancient GREECE,
are commonly known, from the *Crowns*,
Triumphs, and other Marks of public and
appointed Regard, beſtowed on the *Victors*
in the *muſical Conteſts*.

27. " ODES and *Hymns* made a Part of
" their domeſtic Entertainment; and the
" Chiefs were proud to ſignalize themſelves,
" by their Skill in *Melody* and *poetic Song*."
—This is generally known; and needs no
particular Proof. It is introduced here,
that

that it may be accounted for: Becaufe it
hath been held a Practice unworthy the
Character of *Legiflators* and *Heroes*, to be
ambitious of *finging* and *playing* on the
Lyre.　But if we examine the Nature of
the ancient Songs of Greece, we fhall
find that the Performance of them was
worthy of the higheft Characters.　It was
ufual for all who were at their Entertainments, firft to fing together the Praifes of
the Gods [*d*]: Then they fung fucceffively,
one by one, holding a Branch of *Myrtle* in
their Hand, which was fent round the Table [*e*].　In later Times, when the *Lyre*
came more into Ufe, *this* Inftrument was
fent round inftead of the *Myrtle;* and in
this Period it was, that their Songs affumed the Name of *Scolia* [*f*].

　　The poetic Songs were chiefly of the
three great Claffes, *religious*, *political*, and
moral.　Of the firft Clafs, Athenæus hath
preferved no lefs than five: One to Pal-
las, one to Ceres, one to Apollo, one
to Pan, and one to all the tutelary Gods
of Athens [*g*].

[*d*] Plut. *Symp.* l. i. q. i.　Athen. *Deip.* l. xv.
[*e*] Plut. ib.　[*f*] Plut. ib. Athen. ib.
[*g*] Athen. ib.

Of the fecond Clafs, the *political*, in which their *Heroes* were celebrated, though not advanced to the Rank of *Gods*, the fame Author hath given us feveral; in which AJAX, TELAMON, HARMODIUS, the *Heroes* who fell at LEIPSYDRION, ADMETUS, the *Olympic* Victors, and others, were celebrated at their private Entertainments [*b*].

Of the third or *moral* Clafs ATHENÆUS hath likewife tranfmitted to us a Collection. Of this Kind we find one upon the *Vanity* and *Mifchiefs* of *Riches*, one upon *Prudence*, one upon the comparative Excellence of the *Goods* of Life; one upon *Friendfhip*, one upon the *Choice* of *Friends*, one upon *falfe Friends*; and a fine one of ARISTOTLE on the *Force of Virtue*, which may be faid in fome Meafure to comprehend all the three Kinds, *religious*, *political*, and *moral*.

Such being the Nature of the old *Grecian Songs*, and the whole Nation having been prepared to perform and liften to them with Reverence by a correfpondent Education; no Wonder that the higheft Characters in the Commonwealth bore a

[*b*] ATHEN. *Deip.* l. xv.

Part

Part in their Performance at private Entertainments : " For their Songs being en-
" riched with the great and important
" Subjects relative to their public State, and
" being the *eſtabliſhed Vehicle* of *Religion,*
" *Morals,* and *Polity ;* nothing could be
" more fuitable to a high Station in the
" Commonwealth, than a Proficiency in
" this *ſublime* and *legiſlative Art."*

28. " When *Muſic* (that is *Melody* and
" *Poem,* thus *united*) had attained to this
" State of relative *Perfection,* it was ef-
" teemed a *neceſſary Accompliſhment :* And
" an Ignorance in this Art was regarded
" as a capital Defect." Of this we have an
Inſtance, even in THEMISTOCLES himſelf,
who was upbraided with his Ignorance in
Muſic [*i*]. The whole Country of *Cynæthe*
laboured under a parallel Reproach [*k*]:
And all the enormous *Crimes* committed
there, were attributed by the neighbouring
States to the *Neglect* of *Muſic.* — What
Wonder? For according to the Delineation
here given of the ancient *Greek Muſic,* their
Ignorance in this noble Art implied a general Deficiency in the three great Articles,

[*i*] CICERO *Tuſc.* l. i. [*k*] ATHENÆUS, POLYBIUS.

of

of a SOCIAL EDUCATION, *Religion, Morals,* and *Polity.*

29. " The Genius of their *Poem* and *Me-*
" *lody* varied along with their Manners."
Of this Truth we have had abundant
Proofs, in the Courfe of this Differtation ;
where we have feen them emerge from the
Rudenefs of barbarous Life, and improve
through the fucceffive Periods of improving
Manners. We fhall foon fee a parallel Decline of thefe noble Arts, arifing from an
equivalent Caufe : For Manners being the
" leading and moft effential Quality of
" Man, All his other Taftes and Acquire-
" ments naturally correfpond with Thefe ;
" and accommodate themfelves to his Man-
" ners, as to their original Caufe."

30. " As every Change of Manners in-
" fluenced their *Poem* and *Melody,* fo by
" a reciprocal Action, every confiderable
" Change in Thefe influenced their Man-
" ners." The Facts which prove this, will
be given in the thirty-fecond Article.   In
the mean Time, the Reafon is evident : For
not only the Paffion for *Novelty* and *Change*
was immediately dangerous to the *Stability*
of *fmall Republics*; but ftill farther, as *poetic Song* was the eftablifhed *Vehicle* of all
the

the great Principles of *Education*, a Change
in *That* inevitably brought on a Change
in *Thefe*.

31. " There was a provident Commu-
" nity, of Principles uncommonly fevere,
" which fixed the *Subjects* and *Movements*
" of *poetic Song* and *Dance*, by *Law*."
This provident Community was that of
SPARTA. The Practice was not peculiar
to this wife though barbarous Commonwealth. It was borrowed from CRETE ;
and came originally from EGYPT ; where
the fame provident Inftitution had taken
Place in earlier Ages.—In that great Fountain of ancient Polity, not only the Art of
Mufic in it's inlarged Senfe, but even that
of *Painting*, was fixed and made unalterable by Law [*l*]. PLATO, who informs us
of This, gives a particular Detail of the
mufical Eftablifhment, which fets the Principle in a clear Light, and corroborates
what is here advanced. " All their Songs
" and Dances are confecrated to the Gods:
" It is ordained, what Sacrifices fhall be
" offered to each Deity, and what *Hymns*
" and *Choirs* fhall be appointed to each Sa-
" crifice : But if any Perfon makes Ufe of

[*l*] PLATO *de Legibus*, l. ii.

" *Hymns*

" *Hymns* or *Choirs* in the Worfhip of the Gods,
" other than what is appointed by *Law*,
" the Priefts and Magiftrates expel him the
" Community [*m*]. " Hence (faith Plato
in another Place) " their *Mufic* (that is,
" their *Poem* and *Melody*) is found to have
" continued *uncorrupted*, and the *fame*, for
" thoufands of Years [*n*]." A Stroke of
Polity, fatal indeed to *Art*, but excellent
with Refpect to the Stability and Duration
of a State. This uncommon Effort of
Egyptian Legiflation the *Spartan* Lawgiver
adopted from Crete ; and by this fevere
Eftablifhment is faid " three Times to have
" faved the State." Innovations were attempted by three different Muficians, Terpander, Timotheus, and Phrynnis
[*o*] : And as the very Sentence of the *Spartan* Senate againft one of thefe Incroachers
on the fevere Simplicity of the Commonwealth is yet preferved ; it may not be
difagreeable to the Reader, to prefent
him with this curious Remnant of Antiquity. " Whereas Timotheus the *Mi-*
" *lefian*, coming into our City, and de-
" fpifing the ancient Mufic ; rejecting alfo

[*m*] *De Leg.* l. vii. [*n*] Ibid. l. ii. [*o*] Athen.
Deip. l. xiv.

" that

" that Melody which arifeth from feven
" Strings ; and fetting off his Mufic by
" a Multiplicity of Strings, and a new
" Species of Melody, corrupts the Ears
" of our Youth ; and inftead of That
" which is legitimate and pure, corrupt-
" ing the *Enharmonic* by new, various,
" and *Chromatic* Sounds ; and being
" called to the *Eleufinian* Myfteries, did
" divulge the Secrets of that Inftitution ;
" —It feemed good to the *Senate* and
" *Rhetors*, that TIMOTHEUS fhould be
" called to Account for thefe Proceed-
" ings ; that he fhould be compelled to
" cut off the four fuperfluous Strings
" from his Lyre, leaving the feven an-
" cient Tones ; and that he be banifhed
" to a Diftance from the City ; that
" hence forward none may dare to in-
" troduce any new and dangerous Cuftom
" in SPARTA ; left the Honour of our
" mufical Contefts fhould be defiled [*p*]."

[*p*] ARATI PHÆNOMENA, *Ed. Oxon.* at the End of
which this Edict is preferved.—The Charge againft TI-
MOTHEUS, of divulging the Secrets of the *Eleufinian My-*
fteries, appears, at firft Sight, to be oddly introduced *here:*
It feems probable, that he had made thefe *Myfteries* the
Subject of his *Songs :* This is the only Explanation that can
give a thorough Propriety and Confiftence to that Part of
the Decree.   In

In this Edict, we fee the jealous Spirit of a Republic, which could only fubfift by a rigorous Simplicity of Manners, and an unalterable Obedience to it's Laws. There hath been much ill-founded Ridicule thrown on the *Spartans* for this Decifion : For if we confider the dangerous Effects of mere *Innovation* in *fmall Republics*, and the clofe Connection between the *Melody* and the *Subject* in ancient *Mufic*, together with the early and continued Application of *Thefe* to the *Education* of their Youth, we fhall find, that in this Inftance the *Spartans* only acted a cautious and confiftent Part. Their Principle was, to admit *no Change* in *Manners*, and therefore *no Change* in *Mufic*. The defigned Innovation of Timotheus, therefore, would have deftroyed the firft leading Principle, the very Genius of their Republic ; and, confequently, muft have been fatal to the Republic itfelf.

32. " In the Commonwealths which " were of more libertine and relaxed Prin- " ciples, and particularly in that of A- " thens, the Corruption of Manners " brought on the *Corruption* of their *Poem* " and *Melody ;* and this *Corruption* of *Poem*
                          " and

" and *Melody* ſtill farther corrupted *Man-*
" *ners;* the Bards, Poets, or Muſicians,
" being the immediate Inſtruments of the
" Corruption." This mutual Influence of
Manners and Muſic on each other hath
been already explained in two preceding
Articles [*q*]. And the Truth of theſe Rea-
ſonings is confirmed by Facts, which
PLATO gives us at large, in the following
moſt remarkable Paſſage.

" The People (of ATHENS) did not in
" former Times controul the Laws, but
" willingly obeyed them. I mean thoſe
" Laws which were made concerning Mu-
" ſic. For Muſic was then preciſely diſtin-
" guiſhed into its ſeveral Kinds: One was
" appropriated to the Supplication and
" Praiſes of the Gods: Theſe were called
" *Hymns.* Another Species was the la-
" menting or pathetic: A third was the
" *Pæan* or Song of Triumph: A fourth
" was the *Dithyrambic;* and a fifth con-
" ſiſted in ſinging ancient *Laws* or *Pro-*
" *verbs* [*r*]. In Theſe and other Subjects
" eſtabliſhed by Law, it was not allowed
" to uſe one Kind of Melody inſtead of

[*q*] Art. 29, 30.   [*r*] See Art. 6.

" another:

" another : Each Kind had it's particular
" Appropriation.   The Power of deciding
" on Thefe, and of condemning in Cafe of
" Difobedience, was not committed to the
" Hiffes and foolifh Clamours of the Mul-
" titude, as is now the Practice : Neither
" was the Liberty of intemperate Praife
" allowed to a noify Croud : This Deci-
" fion was left to Men diftinguifhed by
" their Senfe and Knowledge ; and a ge-
" neral Silence was maintained, till they
" had heard the Conclufion of the Work.
" The young Men, their Governors, and
" all the People, were obedient to the
" Motions of a Wand.   While this good
" Order was maintained, the Multitude
" willingly obeyed, nor dared to decide
" any thing in a tumultuous Manner.
" But in Courfe of Time the Poets them-
" felves were acceffary to a fatal Change
" in Mufic : They wanted not Genius ;
" but had no Regard to what was juft
" and legitimate ; running into Extrava-
" gance, and too much indulging the
" Vein of Pleafure.   Hence they con-
" founded all the feveral Kinds together;
" affirming that *mere Tafte* and *Pleafure*,
" whether it were that of a *good* or a

L.   " *wicked*

" *wicked* Man, was the only *Criterion* of
" *Mufic*.   In Confequence of this, they
" compofed   their   *Poems*   on   the   fame
" Principle ;   and thus rendered the *Mul-*
" *titude* fo *bold* and *daring* againft the *ef-*
" *tablifhed Mufic*,   that they affumed to
" themfelves the fole Right of deciding
" on it.   Hence the Theatres began to
" be in Uproar, where formerly Silence
" had reigned :   And thus the Privilege
" of *judging* fell from the *Rulers* of the
" State to the *Dregs* of the People.   Had
" this Authority been affumed by the
" *liberal* Part of the City, no great Harm
" had followed :   But now, from this *cor-*
" *rupt Change* in *Mufic*, a *general Licen-*
" *tioufnefs* of *Opinion* hath enfued.—The
" Confequence of this hath been, that
" we no longer are difpofed to obey the
" Magiftrate :   Hence too, that other Evil
" flows,   that we defpife the Authority
" and Precepts of our Parents,   and the
" Advice   and   Wifdom   of   Old   Age.
" And as we are rifing towards the Ex-
" treme of this Corruption, we now re-
" fufe Obedience to the Laws :   And to
" fill up the Meafure of our Iniquities,
" all

" all *Religion* and mutual *Faith* are *loft*
" among us [*s*].

Such is the Picture which the philofophic PLATO hath left of his Time and
Country, a Picture too well confirmed by
the concurrent Teftimony of XENOPHON
[*t*] ; in whofe Accounts, together with
thofe of PLUTARCH [*u*], we fhall foon
fee a particular Delineation of the Progrefs of this Evil, which PLATO here
defcribes in general Terms. [*w*].

L 2   23. " In

[*s*] *De Legibus*, l. iii.
[*t*] See below, Sect vii. Art. 5.   [*u*] See ib.
[*w*] Let us conclude this Article with the Explanation
of a Subject, which hath not hitherto been clearly
treated of, for want of a juft Idea of the ancient *Greek
Mufic.*   The learned VOSSIUS thus expreffeth himfelf :
" It is a doubtful Point, whether we fhould fay, that
" on a Change of Mufic, a Change of Manners enfues ;
" or that a Change in Manners produceth a Change in
" Mufic : The firft was DAMON's Opinion which PLATO
" follows : But CICERO leans to the latter Syftem [*x*]."
On this Paffage it is neceffary firft to obferve, that both
VOSSIUS and CICERO ufe the Word *Mufic* in its *modern* Acceptation, as implying mere *Melody.*   No Wonder, therefore, if they had but an imperfect Comprehen-
fion of PLATO's Argument.   Secondly, On the Principles delivered in this Differtation, it will appear, that
PLATO was of both thefe Opinions, " That Manners
" influenced Mufic, and Mufic influenced Manners."

[*x*] VOSSIUS.

In

33. " In Confequence of thefe Progref-
"fions, a gradual and total *Separation* of
" the *Bard's complex Charatter* enfued. The
" *Leader* of the *State* no longer was am-
" bitious of the poetic and mufical Art;
" nor the *Poet* defcended to the Profeffion
" of *Lyrift*, *Singer*, or *Actor*: Becaufe thefe
" Profeffions, which in the earlieft Ages
" had been the Means of inculcating every
" thing *laudable* and *great*, grew by De-

In the Paffage which VOSSIUS refers to, where the
Opinion of DAMON is delivered, PLATO fpeaks of a
Change in Mufic, as influencing the Manners of a
Commonwealth : This Change he regards, as opening a
Door for Confufion and Novelty in an Affair of public
Confequence ; fimilar to a Neglect of Reverence to old
Men, Parents, or Magiftrates, or any other ancient
and approved Cuftoms that were connected with the
public Welfare : And in this Refpect, the *Influence* of
the *Greek Mufic*, as now explained, on the Manners of
Mankind is too evident to need any farther Proof.

On the other Hand, it is no lefs evident, that PLATO
was of Opinion, that a Corruption of Manners muft corrupt Mufic. He hath fhewn us in the Paffage given
above, that the Boldnefs and Degeneracy of the People
of ATHENS firft allured the Poets to debafe their Art,
by finging fuch Poems as were accommodated to their
vicious Tafte founded on their vicious Manners : That
as Manners had thus debafed Mufic, fo this corrupt Mufic
by a natural Reaction ftill farther corrupted Manners, and
compleated the Deftruction of Religion and Virtue.

" grees

" grees of lefs and lefs Importance ; and
" being at length perverted to the *con-*
" *trary Purpofes*, were in the End *difdained*
" by the wife and virtuous." Thefe gradual Separations of the fevcral Branches
of the Bard's complex Office, and of Melody, Dance, and Song, are not incurious
in their Progreffion.—We have feen, that
in the *earlieft* Ages, the *Gods* or *Legifla-*
tors themfelves often affumed the full and
complex Charaéter; that they were *Poets,*
Lyrifts, Singers, and *Dancers.* The *Dance*
feems firft to have been feparated from
the *Melody* and *Song,* being foon heightened into the *Gymnaftic* Art. The *Le-*
giflators by Degrees quitted the fevcral
Parts of the *Bard's* Charaéter ; a Separation which naturally arofe from decreafing Enthufiafm, and increafing Cares
of Government. As LINUS and ORPHEUS
were the firft, fo PYTHAGORAS and SOLON
feem to have been the laft, who *compofed*
Songs and *fung* them to the furrounding
People.—The Profeffion of *Bard* was now
become a *fecondary* but *refpeétable* Character, as being an Affiftant to the Magiftrate, and an ufeful Servant of the
State, a Teacher of Religion and Morals.

　　　　　　　The

The Bard *fung* and *played*, and led
the *Dance* occafionally : But when Ho-
MER's Poems had eclipfed every other
Epic Strain, another Separation followed : The *Rhapfodifts* arofe in GREECE :
They fung HOMER's Poems to large furrounding Audiences : They were ftrictly
his *Reprefentatives*, who now gave his
Poems to the People, with that poetic
Fire and Rapture which the Bard himfelf had poffeffed and exerted : For in
PLATO's *Ion*, the *Rhapfodift* fays, that
" when he fings a piteous Tale, his Eyes
" fwim in Tears ; when he fings a ter-
" rible Event, his Heart beats, and his
" Hair ftands erect." In the earlier Ages
of Tragedy, the Poet both acted and
fung : But in the Time of SOPHOCLES,
another Separation, parallel to the laft,
enfued ; and the Province of *Actor* began
to be diftinct from that of *Poet*.—Soon
after this Time we find in the Paffage
quoted above from PLATO, that a Separation of the *whole* Art of *Mufic* from
it's *proper Ends* took Place at ATHENS :
It's falutary Effects were now loft : and
as at this Period the Paffion for illiberal *Comedy* (the Species of *corrupt Poe-*
try

try which PLATO hints at) came on, fo
we learn from the concurrent Teftimony of PLUTARCH [*y*] and other
Authors [*z*], that the Exhibition of the
Dramatic Shews at ATHENS had now
degenerated into mere external *Pomp*,
equally expenfive and pernicious. The
fame refpectable Ancient affures us, that
the *Dance*, which had formerly been feparated from the *Song* for warlike Purpofes, was now corrupted by the *Mimes*
in a very extraordinary Degree [*a*]. The
Confequence of thefe Corruptions foon
fhewed themfelves in a fubfequent Period : Hence in the Age of PLATO, another Separation had come on : For now
the complex Name of ᾠδὸς or *Bard* was
difufed and that of ποιητὴς or *Poet* had
affumed it's Place : And as the *Legiflator's* Office had formerly been feparated
from the *Bard's* ; fo now, in Confequence
of this Corruption, and as a natural Effect
of Mufic's finking into a mere *Amufement*,
the *Poet*'s Character became quite diftinct
from that of *Chorift*, *Actor*, or *Dancer*,
and thefe diftinct from each other [*b*].

[*y*] *Sympof.* l. vii. [*z*] JUSTIN, l. vi. [*a*] *Sympof.*
l. ix. q. 15. [*b*] PLATO *de Repub.* l. ii.

L 4   For

For the *moral* End being now *forgot*, and nothing but *Amusement* attended to, a higher Proficiency in these Arts became necessary, and consequently a more severe Application to each.—We must now go back a little, to catch the Rise of another Separation : An *Inroad* was made into the *Muse's Territories :* The public musical Contentions admitted *Prose*, as an Aspirant to the Palm originally due to *Poetry* and *Song*. HERODOTUS was the first who was crowned for *writing* and *speaking* (or more properly for *singing*) *History* at the public Contest [c]. And it is remarkable, that although He brought down the *poetic Song* to the *prosaic* Manner, yet still his Work retained the *fabulous Air*, as well as the *Appellation* of the *Muses :* All which Circumstances, considered in Union, may lead us to the true *poetic* and *fabling* Genius of his celebrated History. THUCIDIDES hints at this Practice in the Beginning of his noble Work [d]: Declaring, that he means it not as a mere Exercise for the *public Contest ;* but as a valuable Possession for *After-Ages.*   In

[c] LUCIAN, HERODOTUS. [d] L. i. c. 6.

later

later Times it became a common Practice for *Sophists* and *Rhetoricians* to contend in *Prose*, at the *Olympic* Games, for
the Crown of Glory [*e*].—The *Delphic
Oracles* kept Pace with these progressive
Separations : In the early Periods they
were delivered by the *Pythia*, with frantic *Gesture*, *Melody*, and *Rythm* [*f*]. In
a succeeding Age, we find the *Pythia*
hath quitted her complex Character ;
Poets are appointed for the Service of
the Temple, and turn the *Oracles* into
Verse : But in the later Times, this Practice had also ceased ; and the *Oracles*
were given in plain Profe [*g*].—In the
Days of ARISTOTLE, a general and almoft a total Separation had taken Place.
The Art of playing on the *Lyre*, which
had been the *Glory* of their early *Legiflators*, was now regarded as a *Reproach*
to a young *King :* The Art of *finging*,
which had once been a diftinguifhed Attribute of their *Gods*, was now reckoned
an ignoble Practice for a *Man* [*h*]: The
Choir of fome of their Dramas gave

[*e*] LUCIAN *de Salt.*   [*f*] Above, Art. viii.
[*g*] STRABO, l. ix. CICERO *de Div.* l. ii.
[*h*] ARISTOT. *Polit.* l. viii. c. 5.

Way

Way to *Melody* merely *inftrumental*, which now firſt aſſumed the Name of *Muſic :* The *Rhapſodiſts* had, about this Time, begun to quit a Part of *Their* Profeſ-ſion; and inſtead of *ſinging*, often *recited* HOMER's Poems [*i*]. To conclude all, the wiſe and learned PLUTARCH in a later Period, viewing the poetic and muſi-cal Entertainments in that corrupt State which they held in his own Time, though he ſtill aſſerts the Uſe of Muſic and Po-etry in private Education, gives up the public Exhibitions, as chiefly fit to gratify the Taſte of an abandoned People [*k*].

S E C T. VI.

Of the Origin and Progreſſion of Comedy in ancient GREECE.

THUS we have attempted to unfold the natural Origin and Progreſs of Poety in ancient GREECE, through it's ſeveral Forms of *Ode*, *Epic*, and *Tragedy ;* and to trace the Gradations of their po-etic and muſical Arts, from the Periods of their Riſe and Power, to thoſe of their Corruption and Decay.

[*i*] ARISTOT. *Poet.* c. 26.
[*k*] *Plut. Sympos.* l. vii. qu. 9.—l. ix. qu. 15.

But

But there is one confiderable Branch of the Poetry of ancient GREECE, I mean COMEDY, the Rife and Progreffion of which, together with their Caufes, have been defignedly paffed in Silence : Becaufe, if this Difquifition had been mixed with what hath been delivered concerning the *Ode*, *Epic*, and *Tragedy*, the Chain of Argument would have been broken ; and that Order and Clearnefs deftroyed, which it was neceffary to preferve as much as poffible in this involved Subject.—Not only fo ; but the Birth and Progrefs of Comedy itfelf (as will appear below) was owing to thofe Corruptions which we have here unfolded : The Hiftory of this Species, therefore, naturally came laft, in the Order of Things.

Let us now proceed, therefore, to reduce the Origin and Progrefs of the *Greek Comedy* to their natural and effential Caufes.—To point out the Rife of this Poem from favage Life ; to unfold the true Reafons why it was fo late in taking it's legitimate Form in GREECE ; and then to explain, on what Foundation the *old*, *middle*, and *new* Comedy, appeared in their refpective *Succeffions*.

In

In the Defcription of the Savage Song-Feafts, given above from LAFITAU, it appears that thefe warlike Tribes " are " ftill quicker at rallying, than at praif-" ing, each other. He who dances, takes " whomfoever he pleafeth by the Hand; " and brings him forth into the midft of " the Affembly; to which he yields with-" out Refiftance. Mean while the Dancer " continued to *fing*, and fometimes in his " Song, and fometimes in the Intervals, " he throws his Sarcafms on the Patient, " who hears him without Reply.—At eve-" ry *bon Mot*, loud Peals of Laughter arife " along the Galleries, who animate this " Sport, and often oblige the Patient to " cover his Head in his Mantle [*l*]."

Now, if we again fuppofe, as we have already done, that the Ufe of *Letters* fhould come among thefe favage Tribes, and be cultivated with that Spirit which is natural to a free and active People; from this Picture, as given by LAFITAU, the following Confequences would naturally arife.

1. " Their cafual Strokes of Raillery " would improve into written Invectives,

[*l*] See above, Sect. li.

" which

" which would occafionally be fung by
" their farcaftic Choirs." Becaufe nothing
could be more alluring to a People of
this fatyric Turn, than fuch a Repofitory
of Wit and Raillery ; which, like a Qui-
ver ftored with the keeneft Arrows, would
be ever at Hand, ready to be difcharged
againft the occafional Objects of their
Refentment.

2. " Narrative or Epic Poems of the
" *invective* or *comic* Kind would likewife
" arife, and be occafionally fung at their
" public Feftivals." For the Spirit of Sarcafm being once awakened, it would of
Courfe proceed from occafional Strokes of
Raillery, to the Recital of ridiculous Actions, for the Gratification and Entertainment of a lively and fatyric People.

3. " From thefe two Species (the *choral*
" and *narrative* united) the firft rude
" Outline of *Comedy* would arife." We
have feen how *Tragedy* arofe from parallel
Caufes : And Thefe would naturally take
Place in producing *Comedy*. For the *Nar-*
rative, already animated by Action, would
eafily flide into dramatic Reprefentation,
as in the Rife of *Tragedy ;* and the correfpondent *Peals of Laughter* (by the Af-
                              fiftance

fiftance of written Invectives) would affume the Form of a *comic Choir.*

4. " While the falutary Principles of
" Legiflation fhould prevail, Comedy thus
" formed, would be little encouraged by
" the Leaders of the State." For the
grander Kinds of Poetry, already treated
of, containing the Principles of Religion,
Polity, and Morals, would draw their
main Attention; while their Comedy, being no more than the Vehicle of Ridicule and vague Invective, would (at moft)
be only *endured* by prudent Legiflators.

5. " A provident Community, of Prin-
" ciples uncommonly fevere, might even
" banifh this Species of Poem, as deftruc-
" tive to their State." Becaufe nothing
could be more dangerous to a Commonwealth eftablifhed on Severity of Manners, than the unbounded Licentioufnefs
of Sentiment and Speech, which this Comedy muft tend to produce.

6. " If in a State of more relaxed Prin-
" ciples, where fuch Comedy had been to-
" lerated, a general Corruption of Manners
" fhould take Place among the People;
" and if by any means, fuch a corrupt
" People fhould over-power the Magif-
                                        " trates,

" ſtrates, and aſſume to themſelves the
" Reins of Government ; then, this Spe-
" cies of Comedy would riſe into Credit,
" and be publicly eſtabliſhed." For the
upright Leaders of the State being *de-
poſed*, and the *Creatures* of ſuch a *corrupt
People* being ſeated in their *Place*, *that
Comedy* would now be *authorized* by Law,
which was moſt accommodated to the
Taſte and *Vices* of ſuch a *corrupt People.*

7. " The Ridicule and Invective of their
" Comedy, thus eſtabliſhed, would be
" pointed chiefly againſt thoſe Magiſ-
" trates, or private Men, whoſe Qualities
" would be hateful to the debauched
" Populace." For Corruption being now
eſtabliſhed as it were by Law ; that is,
by the Voice of a degenerate People
which ſtood in the Place of Law ; the
Poets would find it neceſſary to gratify
the People's Vices as the ſureſt Road to
Succeſs ; and the moſt certain Road to
this muſt be by the *Ridicule of Virtue.*

8. " If a *Tyranny* ſhould ſuddenly erect
" itſelf on the Ruins of ſuch a People,
" it would by it's Authority *ſilence* this
" Species of *Comedy.*"—For every thing
hateful to the People being now the eſtabliſhed

tablifhed Subject of the comic Mufe, the Tyrants, who had taken away the public Liberty, muft expect to become the Subject of Comedy, if permitted to revel in its former Licentioufnefs.

9. " The Poets would probably find " a Subterfuge, for the Gratification of " the People ; and continue to reprefent " *real. Characters* under *feigned Names.*" For this would be the only Species of Comedy they could purfue with a Probability of Succefs : And this might be continued without much Danger, if they were cautious with Refpect to the Perfons of the Tyrants.

10. " If a great Conqueror fhould arife, "'and, by fubduing a Variety of Nati- " ons, fhould open a Communication be- " tween fuch a State and others of more " luxurious and refined Manners, this *fe-* " *cond* Species of Comedy would naturally " receive a *Polifh* ; and, inftead of the " indirect perfonal Invective, would af- " fume the more delicate Form of gene- " ral Raillery, and become a Picture of " human Life."—For one of the firft Efforts of a growing Politenefs is to avoid all Occafions of *Offence* ; and this, without

Refpect

Refpect to any Confequences, either good
or bad, which may affect the Public ; but
merely from a felfifh Regard to the Opinion of *Elegance,* and the Pride of *Urbanity.*

In Support of thefe Deductions, let us
now endeavour to *realize* them; by fhewing, that fuch Confequences did arife in
GREECE: And in the Courfe of this Argument, the Writer hopes he fhall be able
to difclofe the true Caufes of the Progreffion of the ancient Comedy, fo different
from that of the higher Kinds of Poetic
Compofition.

1. " In the earlieft Periods of the Greek
" States, their Cafual Strokes of Raillery
" were improved into written Invectives,
" and were occafionally fung by their far-
" caftic Choirs." Thefe written Invectives
were in Fact fo early, that all the Greek
Writers with one Voice confefs themfelves
altogether ignorant of their Origin. Their
firft Appearance is afcribed by different
Authors to different Nations [*m*]; and no
Wonder if Evidence be wanting in Support
of each Pretence, when it is propable, that·

[*m*] See VOSSIUS *Inft. Poët.* l. ii. c. 23.

M   thefe

thefe farcaftic Choirs arofe in many of the *Greek* States nearly at the fame Time ; that is, in or about the firft Periods of Civilization and Letters. . For we have feen, that fuch a Period would naturally produce them : " Becaufe nothing could be " more alluring to a People of the fatyric " Turn, than fuch a Repofitory of Rail- " lery and Sarcafm."　However, we muft not omit to obferve, that their Traditions are much more accommodated to Nature and Probability on this Subject, than on the Rife of the tragic Choir, which they feem generally to have attributed to the fingle Practice of the drunken Votaries of BACCHUS.

2. " Narrative or Epic Poems of the in- " vective or comic Kind arofe, and were " occafionally fung at their public Fefti- " vals."　For the Truth of this Fact we have the Teftimony of ARISTOTLE, who tells us, " that although we know not the " Names either of thefe Poems or their " Authors ; yet there is Reafon to believe " that many had been written before Ho- " MER ; and that his *Margites* brought " this Species to its Perfection in the fame " Manner as the *Iliad* and *Odyffy* had
" com-

" compleated the Form of the Epic Po-
" em [n]." That HOMER, as well as other
Bards of the early Periods, fung their comic Poems at the feftal Solemnities, needs
no farther Proof here.

3. " From thefe two Species (the *Choral*
" and *Narrative* united) the firft rude
" Outline of Comedy arofe." The *Narra-*
tive, already animated by a lively Action,
did eafily flide into *dramatic* Reprefentation;
and the correfpondent Peals of *Laughter*
excited among the furrounding Audience,
by means of written Invectives, affumed
the Form of the *comic Choir.* In this
Point, we have again to contend with the
general Body of Critics, from ARISTOTLE
down to the prefent Times, who all con-
cur in afcribing the Rife of the legitimate
Form of Comedy to HOMER's *Margites;*
in the fame Manner as they have afcribed
the Rife of *Tragedy* to the *Iliad* and *Odyſſy.*
But notwithftanding this general Concur-
rence of Opinion, it feems evident that the
Progreffion of Comedy was founded in the
fame Caufes with that of Tragedy: That
they both naturally arofe in the Courfe of

[n] *Poët,* c. 4.

Things

Things, from an Union of the *Narration* and the *Choir*, without any Refpect had to HOMER's Poems. The fame Arguments that have proved the one, will confirm the other. We fee the natural Seeds of Comedy and fcenic Reprefentation in favage Life, no lefs than thofe of Tragedy [o]: Nay, even in the earlieft Periods of GREECE itfelf, we fhall find the firft rude Form of Comedy, arifing from an Union of *dramatic Reprefentation* and a *Choir*, long before HOMER exifted. In the Account already cited from STRABO and others, of the *mufical Conteft* eftablifhed at DELPHI, which in Time branched out into the equeftrian and gymnaftic Games, as we have found the firft rude Form of *Tragedy;* fo now we fhall find likewife a faint Outline of the firft rude Form of *Comedy.* For it appears, that APOLLO with his Choir, and his Worfhippers, in after-times, not only reprefented his Victory, and fung a Pæan in Confequence of it (in which Union we fee the firft rude Form of Tragedy) but likewife, in the Way of Ridicule they reprefented the *Hiffes* of the dying Serpent, and fung an *In-*

[o] See above, Sect. ii.

vective

vective or *Sarcafm* on his Overthrow [*p*].
For fo I underftand the Word ιαμϛος and
ιαμϛιζιιν, ufed by thefe ancient Writers on
this Occafion; as implying only *Sarcaftic
Verfes*, and not *Iambics* in the ftrict Senfe;
which are generally believed to have been
firft formed by ARCHILOCHUS, many
Ages after the Fact here alluded to. And
hence the true Reafon appears, why the
Greek Comedy was written in *Verfe;* becaufe it was originally *fung.*—Now, in
this Union of *comic Reprefentation* and a
fatyrical Choir, we fee the genuine, though
imperfect and *rude Form* of the *old Greek
Comedy*.

4. " While the falutary Principles of
" Legiflation prevailed, Comedy, thus
" formed, was little encouraged by the
" Leaders of the State." The Authority
of ARISTOTLE is clear and decifive on
this Point. " Comedy remained obfcure
" and unknown, becaufe little Regard was
" had to it from the Beginning; the Ma-
" giftrate being late in appointing it a
" Choir." He affigns no Reafon ·for this
Conduct of the Magiftrate: But a fuffi-

[*p*] See the Authors cited above, Sect. v. Art. 17.

cient

cient Reafon appears to be given above.
" For the grander Kinds of Poetry con-
" taining the Principles of Religion, Po-
" lity, and Morals, drew their main At-
" tention; while their Comedy, being no
" more than the Vehicle of Ridicule and
" vague Invective, was only *endured* by
" prudent Legiflators." The Truth of this
Article will receive Confirmation from the
two fucceeding.

5. " There was a provident Community,
" of Principles uncommonly fevere, which
" even banifhed this Species of Poem, as
" deftructive to their State." We have already feen the Providence and Caution of
the *Spartans* in regulating their *Mufic* for
the Security of their Republic [*q*]. We
fhall now fee the admirable Confiftency of
their Conduct, with Refpect to the very
Beginnings of *Comedy*, when it firft dawned
among them in the Verfes of ARCHILO-
CHUS. " The *Spartans* ordered the Wri-
" tings of ARCHILOCHUS to be banifhed
" from their City, becaufe they thought
" the Perufal of them was dangerous to
" the Purity of Manners. They did not
" chufe that the Minds of their Children

[*q*] See above.

fhould

" fhould be tainted with them, left they
" fhould more hurt their Morals, than
" fharpen their Wit [*r*]."

6. " In the Republic of ATHENS, which
" was of more relaxed Principles, where
" this Comedy had been tolerated, a gene-
" ral Corruption of Manners took Place
" among the People: The corrupt People
" over-powered the Magiftrates; affumed
" to themfelves the Reins of Government,
" and on this Foundation the old Comedy
" arofe into Credit, had a Choir appointed
" by the Magiftrate, and was publicly ef-
" tablifhed." This was the natural and
neceffary Confequence of the Power of a
corrupt People.   For the upright Magiftrates being depofed, and the Creatures
of this corrupt People feated in their Place,
that Comedy was now authorized by Law,
which was moft accommodated to the Vices
and Tafte of a diffolute Populace.

[*r*] VAL. MAX. l. vi. c. 3.—In After-times, when
the fevere Manners and the Glory of this Republic funk
together, we find its Conduct altogether correfpondent
with thefe Principles.   The *Mimes*, the moft diffolute
Species of Comedy, were then admitted.   See SUIDAS,
ATHENÆUS, and other Authors of the later Periods.

M 4   Thefe

Thefe Caufes clearly account for the Eftablifhment of the old Comedy, at that very Period when it took Place. But as other Caufes, void of all Foundation, have been affigned for this, by various Authors; it will be neceffary to prove the Truth of the Caufes here alledged, from the Authority of the Greek Writers.

PLATO, in the Paffage cited above [*s*], gives us the Hiftory of the Corruption of the People, and of Mufic ; but in fuch general Terms, that, without fome farther Evidence, it is impoffible clearly to fix the Time when, or the Means by which, this Change was brought about, fo fatal to the Republic of *Athens*. It happens fortunately, that PLUTARCH hath recorded the Event with fuch Particularity of Circumftance, as leaves no Room to doubt on this Subject. PERICLES was the Man, who for his own private Ends of Popularity, effected this ruinous Change : For " By giving the People the Plunder and " Poffeffion of the Lands taken from the " Enemy, and by fquandering the public " Monies (formerly referved for the Ufes " of War) in SHEWS and PLAYS for their

[*s*] See Sect. v. Art. 34.

" *Enter-*

" *Entertainment*, and by Grants of Lar-
" geffes and Penfions, he changed them
" from a fober, modeft, and thrifty Peo-
" ple who maintained themfelves by their
" own Labour, into a riotous and de-
" bauched Multitude ; and thus roufed
" them into Sedition againft the Court
" of the *Areopagus* [*t*]." From this Paffage it is evident, that Pericles not
only debauched the *Athenian* People ; but
that the Exhibition of Plays and Shews
was one of the very ·Engines of Corruption [*u*].—The concurrent Teftimony
of Xenophon clears the whole Affair ;

[*t*] *In Pericle.*
·[*u*] Thus Cicero fpeaks of the old Greek Comedy.—" Efto: populares Homines, improbos, in Rem-
" publicam feditiofos, *Cleonem, Cleophontem, Hyperbolum*
" læfit:—Patiamur:—Sed Periclem, cum jam fuæ
" Civitati maxima Auftoritate plurimos annos Domi et
" Bello præfuiffet, violari Verfibus, et eos agi in Scena,
" non plus decuit, quam fi *Plautus* nofter voluiffet, aut
" *Nævius*, P. et *Cn. Scipioni*, aut *Cæcilius M. Catoni*
" maledicere." Ex Frag. Cic. de Rep. l. iv.—Where,
we may obferve, the Judgment of Cicero is falfe concerning Pericles: As it appears, that he was the firft
Corrupter of the People: And it feems to have been a
juft Punifhment, that he was lafhed by that illiberal Comedy, which His own Influence firft let in upon the
State.

and

and gives us a full View of the Confequences of this general Corruption, fo
far as the *old Comedy* is concerned. For
in his Difcourfe on the *Athenian* Republic, he informs us, 1*ß*, That, at the Period we have now fixed, " The Body of
" the People expelled All Good Men from
" the Magiftracy, and advanced wicked
" Men in their Places." 2*dly*, That " they
● gave the Practice and Profit of the *mu-*
" *fical Exercifes* to the Dregs of the Peo-
" ple." 3*dly*, That " in their Comedies
" they fuffered none to be ridiculed, but
" thofe of higher Station and Worth ;
" unlefs one of their own Rank happened
" to diftinguifh himfelf from the Multi-
" tude ; and then he became the Object
" of theatrical Derifion [*w*]."

Thefe Evidences are fo clear and precife, as to leave no Foundation of a Doubt
on this Subject.

Lord SHAFTESBURY hath greatly miftaken this Matter in his *Advice to an Au-*
thor [*x*]; and is as carelefs or defective
here in the Circumftance of Erudition, as
at other Times in that of Reafoning. He

[*w*] XENOPHON *de Rep.* ATHEN.
[*x*] *Characteriftics,* vol. i.

feems

- feems in one Paffage to attribute the late
Cultivation and Eftablifhment of the old
Comedy to it's being of more *difficult* Compofition than Tragedy: " In this Part (Tra-
" gedy) the Poets fucceeded fooner than in
" Comedy, or the facetious Kind ; as it was
" natural indeed to fuppofe, fince this was
" in reality the eafieft (eafier) Manner of
" the two." This is deciding a doubtful
Point by a mere Affirmation : For the
comparative Difficulty of thefe two Kinds
hath been treated at large by a learned
and moft judicious Writer, who after a
candid and profound Difcuffion of the
Queftion, thinks it beft to leave it unde-
cided [y]. The noble Writer, next, feems
to

---

[y] BRUMOY *Theatre des Grecs,* tom. vi.—This
Queftion hath indeed been faid, by a learned Writer, to admit of a *decifive Anfwer,* on this Principle ; that " Tragedy, whofe End is the *Pathos,* pro-
" duces it by *Action,* while Comedy produces it's End,
" the *Humorous,* by *Character.* Now it is much more
" difficult to *paint Manners,* than to *plan Action ;* be-
" caufe That requires the *Philofopher's Knowledge* of
" *human Nature ;* this, only the *Hiftorian's Knowledge*
of *human Events.*"—But in the Courfe of this Argument, it feems entirely forgot, that the tragic Poet's
Province is not only to *plan,* but to *paint* too. Had
he no farther Tafk, than what depends on the mere
Hiftorian's

to attribute the late Cultivation of Comedy to " the Spirit of literary Criti-
" cifm, which in the Nature of Things
" could not arife, till it had Materials
" to work on ; and This he fuppofeth to
" have been the *falfe Sublime* of their
" *Tragedies,* which were often *parodied* in
" the *old Comedy.*—But neither can this
Caufe be fufficient to account for the
Effect ; becaufe it appears that the beft
Men, as well as the beft Tragedies, were
parodied or ridiculed more commonly

Hiftorian's Knowledge of *human Events,* the Reafoning
would hold.   But as it is the firft and moft effential
Effort of his Genius, in the Conftruction of a *compleat*
Tragedy, to *invent* and *order* a *pathetic* Plan, *confiftent*
in all it's Parts, and *rifing* towards it's *Completion* by
a *Succeffion* of Incidents which may *keep up* and conti-
nually *increafe Terror* or *Pity ;* it is manifeft, that the
Perfection of his *Plan* depends not on his mere *hiftoric
Knowledge* of *human Events,* but on his *philofophic Difcernment* of *human Paffions ;* aided by a *warm* and
enlarged Invention : Talents as rare, at leaft, as the
Knowledge or *Difcernment* of *human Characters.*—If to
this we add the fubfequent Tafk, of giving the *high
Colourings* of *Paffion* to the tragic *Plan* thus *ordered,*
the *Difficulty* of writing a compleat *Tragedy* may feem
to be in fome Refpects *equal,* in others *fuperior* to that
of producing a compleat *Comedy :* For in the *Conduct* of
this laft Species, it is acknowledged, that a *fmall Degree* of *poetic Invention* will *fupport* it.

than

than the worſt.   Of this, the Fate of
Socrates may ſtand as a convincing
Proof. This Faƈt could not entirely eſ-
cape the Notice of the noble Writer ;
for he acknowledges, that " even this
" *Remedy* itſelf was found to turn into
" a *Diſeaſe* [z]."   But we have already
proved, that it was a Diſeaſe even on
it's firſt Appearance.   In a Word, the
Authorities given above, in Support of
the true Cauſes of the Cultivation and
Eſtabliſhment of the old Greek Comedy
at Athens, contain the cleareſt Proof
that the noble Writer's Deduƈtions on
this Subjeƈt are *ſpecious*, but *not ſolid ;*
and that he diſcovers but little of what
he ſeems to value ſo much, " a Compre-
" henſion of ancient Manners and ancient
" Hiſtory."—But what is odd enough,
after having ſeparately aſſigned theſe fictitious Cauſes, as being each the Foundation on which the old Comedy aroſe and
was eſtabliſhed, He at length glances ac-
cidentally upon the true one : Yet manifeſtly without any particular Knowledge
of the Faƈts which ſupport it.   " Ac-
" cording to this *Homerical* Lineage of

[z] P. 248.

                              " Poetry,

" Poetry, *Comedy* would naturally prove
" the *Drama* of *lateſt Birth.* For though
" ARISTOTLE cites HOMER's *Margites* as
" analogous to *Comedy,* yet the *Iliad* and
" *Odyſſy,* in which the heroic Style pre-
" vails, having been ever *higheſt in Eſ-*
" *teem,* were likeſt to be *firſt wrought*
and cultivated [a]." We may conclude,
then, upon the Authority of the three
great Ancients cited above, that " the
" Cultivation and *Eſtabliſhment* of the
" old *Greek Comedy* aroſe from the united
" *Corruption* and *Power* of the *Athenian*
" People."

7. " The Ridicule and Invective of their
" Comedy, thus eſtabliſhed, was pointed
" chiefly againſt thoſe Magiſtrates or pri-
" vate Men, whoſe Qualities were hate-
" ful to the debauched Populace." For
the Proof of this, the Reader is referred
to the Paſſages already cited from PLATO,
and XENOPHON: And on this Solution,
the Fate of SOCRATES is clearly accounted for. Nor could any thing be
more natural, if the Cauſes here aſſigned
for the Eſtabliſhment of the old Comedy

[a] *Characteriſtics,* vol. i. p. 253. Notes.

be

be true. " For Corruption being now
" eftablifhed, as it were, by Law : that is,
" by the Voice of a degenerate People,
" which ftood in the Place of Law ; the
" Poets found it neceffary to gratify the
" People's Vices as the fureft Road to
" Succefs ; and the only Road to this,
" was now by the *Ridicule* of *Virtue.*

8. " A Tyranny fuddenly erected itfelf
" on the Ruins of the corrupt *Athenian*
" People, and at once filenced this Spe-
" cies of Comedy." This Event happened on the taking of Athens by Ly-
sander ; and through the Authority of
the thirty Tyrants whom he eftablifhed
there. Thefe *Oppreffors* did That from
Fear, which *upright* Magiftrates would
have done from *Virtue.* The plain Reafon hath been affigned above : " Becaufe
" every thing hateful to the People being
" now the eftablifhed Subject of the co-
" mic Mufe, the Tyrants who had de-
" ftroyed the public Liberty, muft expect
" to become the Subject of Comedy, if
" permitted to revel in it's former Li-
" centioufnefs." Here again the noble
Author of the Characteriftics feems to
affign a fictitious Caufe for this Event,

                                    drawn

drawn from his own Conjectures, inftead
of Hiftory. "Nothing could have been
" the Caufe of this gradual Reform in
" the Commonwealth of Wit, befide the
" real Reform of Tafte and Humour in
" the Commonwealth or Government it-
" felf."—For, faith he, " it *little concerned*
" the *Foreigners in Power* (the thirty Ty-
" rants) after what Manner thofe *Citizens*
" treated *one another* in their *Comedies*;
" or what Sort of Wit or Humour they
" made Choice of, for their ordinary Di-
" verfions [*b*]." It can hardly be neceffary to point out, in what Circumftance
this Reafoning is defective. Had the private Citizens buffooned *each other only* in
their *Comedies*, the *Thirty Tyrants* would
indeed have had little to fear : But as it
is evident, that the *public Magiftrates*, and
their *Conduct*, had been the ftanding Objects of theatrical Ridicule, it certainly
much concerned thefe *Foreigners in Power*,
to prevent that farcaftic Reprefentation of
their oppreffive Government, which they
muft neceffarily expect from the keen
Spirit of an exafperated and licentious

[*b*] *Characteriftics*, vol. i p 250. 249.

People.

People. The noble Writer endeavours to confirm his Opinion by a parallel Inftance drawn from the *Roman* Commonwealth ; where a fimilar Prohibition took Place with regard to the *Atellane* Fables, at a Time, when no Effects of foreign " Power, or of a home Tyranny can be " pretended [*c*]." But this Inftance joined to the Evidences already given on the Subject, inftead of confirming, overturns his Syftem : It only proves what was alledged above, that the *Athenian Tyrants* did that from *Fear*, which the *Roman Magiftrates* did from *Virtue*.

9. " The Poets found a Subterfuge, for " the Gratification of the People ; and " continued to reprefent real Characters " under feigned Names." Thus the *middle Comedy* was naturally eftablifhed. For this was the only Species which they could now purfue with any Probability of *Succefs :* And this was continued without much *Danger*, as we find they were cautious, with Refpect to the Perfons of the Tyrants.—That fuch was the true Origin of this Change in the Character

[*c*] P. 251.

N   of

of the Greek Comedy, appears farther
from the two following Confiderations.
Firſt, there is not the leaſt Reaſon to
believe the Athenian People were at all
changed from their coarſe Manners and
profligate Character, at the Time when
the old Comedy was ſilenced : And ſe-
condly, by the Accounts left concerning
the Genius of the *middle Comedy*, it appears,
that it was in all Reſpects as illiberal
and buffooning, in it's Beginnings, as the
old Comedy had been ; the ſingle Circumſtance of *nominal Deſignation* only excepted.

10. " A great *Conqueror* aroſe : And, by
" ſubduing a Variety of Nations, opened
" a *Communication* between the Common-
" wealth of ATHENS, and the *eaſtern*
" Kingdoms which were of more *luxurious*
" and *refined* Manners : On this Event,
" the *ſecond* or *middle* Species of *Comedy*
" naturally received a *Poliſh* ; and, lay-
" ing aſide the indirect perſonal Invective,
" aſſumed the more delicate Form of ge-
" neral Raillery ; and became a Picture
" of human Life." The learned Reader
will eaſily ſee, that ALEXANDER *the*
Great is the Conqueror here alluded to:

in

in his Reign it was, and not till that late
Period, that the *middle* Comedy was polifhed into the *new*. This was the natural Effect of that Politenefs, which was
introduced at ATHENS by a frequent and
familiar Commerce with the effeminate
Nations of the Eaft. Till then, although
the *Athenians* juftly boafted a Superiority
in the *Arts*, yet in their Converfe and
Treatment of each other, the concurrent
Authority of ancient Hiftorians, as well
as the more certain Teftimony of their
own remaining Comedies affure us, that
they were of an *illiberal* and *buffooning*
Turn. But no fooner were the *Afiatic*
Luxuries and Refinements brought to
ATHENS, by the Conquefts of ALEXAN-
DER, than their coarfe Manners melted
gradually into falfe Politenefs and Effe-
minacy. Now, " one of the firft Effects
" of a growing Politenefs, is to avoid all
" Occafions of Offence ; and this, with-
" out Refpect to any Confequences, either
" good or bad, which may affect the
" Public ; but merely from a felfifh Re-
" gard to the Opinion of *Elegance*, and
" the Pride of *Urbanity*."

N 2

This

This Reasoning coincides in all Re-
spects with the last Progression of Comedy at ATHENS: And those Writers,
as Lord SHAFTESBURY and the Author
of the Life of HOMER, who have attempted to resolve the Establishment of
the new Comedy into a *Reform* or *Improvement* of Manners, in a *virtuous* Sense,
have mistaken *Shadows* for *Realities*, and
confounded *Decency* with *Virtue*. For it is
certain, that both private and public Virtue were at the lowest Ebb, while Comedy was assuming it's *new* and finished
Form. This we are assured of by the
concurrent Testimony of PLUTARCH,
JUSTIN, and other ancient Writers: Even
so far were the *Athenians* from regarding
the public Welfare or Defence of their
Country, that it was made a capital
Crime for any Man to propose the Re-
establishment of their Militia, or the Application of the public Funds to it's Maintenance [*d*]. Their Vices therefore were
not *lessening*, but *refining :* And the Idea
of *Decency* was sliding in, to supplant
the rougher Appearances of *Virtue*. We

[*d*] LIBANIUS *Arg.* ad OLYNTH. I.

know

know a neighbour Nation, in which parallel Effects prevail: a Nation who are too
generally " licentious in private Morals,
" though in public Conduct decent :" And
it is remarkable, that from this Refinement in Vices, a Species of Manners and
of Comedy, there prevails, altogether fimilar to thofe of the later *Greeks.* For while
their private Converfation abounds with
Irreligion, Immorality, and *Obfcenity,* nothing is admitted on their Stage, but
what is confiftent with *Piety, good Morals,* and *good Breeding.*

Such, then, was the Rife, Progrefs, and
Completion, of *Comedy* in ancient GREECE.
And fo far muft be allowed, that although
the *Caufes* of this gradual Reform do not
challenge much Commendation ; yet upon
the whole, the *Effect* was *good.* For from
thefe Caufes arofe the elegant and fault-
lefs MENANDER ; whofe Writings, in After-Times, became the Object of all polite
Converfations, and the *Standard* of *good
Breeding,* in the Days of PLUTARCH [e].

As to the *dramatic Satyr* and the *Mimes*
of ancient GREECE, they do not properly

[e] *Sympof.* L. vii. qu. 8.

N 3   merit

merit a particular Confideration in this Work. The *firſt* (if we may judge from the only remaining Model, the *Cyclops* of EURIPIDES) feems to have been no more than a drolling, grotefque, and *comic* Reprefentation of their *ſylvan Demi-Gods* and *Heroes:* The *ſecond* no more than an irregular, obfcene, and licentious *Farce.* Their *Riſe,* therefore, is naturally included in That of *Comedy:* and as to their *Progreſ-ſions* we know nothing of them.

S E C T.   VII.

Of the Riſe and Progreſs of the paſtoral *Species.*

IT will appear at large hereafter [*f*], that the Manners of Savages depend more on the *Barrenneſs* or *Fertility* of their *Soil,* than on the mere Influences of *Climate, Heat,* or *Cold.* The *Wants* that ariſe from a barren Soil, and the Methods of *Violence* neceſſary to relieve them, naturally pro-duce the *ferocious* Character. The ſpon-taneous Productions of a fertile Soil bring an *unſought* Relief to the Wants of it's In-

[*f*] In the Work advertiſed at the End of this Volume.

habi-

habitants : hence their Character is naturally *indolent* and *peaceful.*

From the *firſt* of theſe *Cauſes* we have
found the natural Origin of the *grand* and
terrible Kinds of Poetry, among the *moun-
tainous* Diſtricts and *warlike* Tribes of
GREECE. . From the *ſecond*, we may naturally expect to find the Origin of the
mild and *peaceful* Paſtoral, in the fertile
Vales of SICILY.

Here indeed it meets us.   Not but that
in other *fertile Spots*, the ſame Species
may have ariſen *ſooner:* But SICILY is
the firſt Scene of Paſtoral, that Hiſtory
hath clearly delivered down to ſucceeding
Times.

DAPHNIS is the moſt ancient Sicilian
Bard of this Kind, that Hiſtory hath recorded.   DIODORUS hath given us a fine
Deſcription of his rural Dwelling; which
appears to have been one of the moſt fertile, and beautiful Spots in SICILY [*g*].
His Condition was ſuitable: for his
Wealth conſiſted in Herds of Cattle
[*h*].   The Hiſtorian placeth him in a
very ancient Period; as far back as the
Age of MERCURY [*i*]. 'Tis therefore pro-

[*g*] L. iv.   [*h*] ib.

bable,

bable, that he gave but the firſt rude
Sketch of the paſtoral Song.   After Him,
a Succeſſion of paſtoral Bards aroſe in
SICILY; whoſe Poems (as well as thoſe
of their Maſter DAPHNIS) have periſhed
in the Wreck of Time.   At laſt, THEOCRI-
TUS appeared ;   in whoſe Paſtorals this
Species appears in it's legitimate and fi-
niſhed Form.

As the Poems of THEOCRITUS are the
chief remaining Models of the Kind, they
are the ſureſt Foundation of our Reaſon-
ings on the Subject : And the Circumſtances which they lead us to, concerning
the Riſe and Progreſs of this Species, are
theſe which follow.

1. They contain internal Proofs, that
the Paſtoral was the natural Produce of
the Fertility of the Iſland.   The principal
Perſons introduced, are all of them the
Chieftains of the paſtoral Tribes: They
are either rich in *Cattle*, *Sheep*, or *Goats*.
The *Place* and *Time* of their Songs are
identified and *fixed :*   The Manners deſcribed are ſimple and natural: The Dia-
lect is ſuited to them: their ancient Bard,
the famed DAPHNIS, is often alluded to:

[i] L. iv.

his

his Amours and Death are fung: In a Word, every Circumftance feems united, that can tend to prove them the artlefs Effufions of a paftoral Enthufiafm, defcribing what it faw and heard.

2. The *natural Union* of *Poem* and *Melody* is here exhibited in its native and fimple State. The *poetic Song* is always accompanied with the *paftoral Pipe*. And it is evident from a Variety of Paffages, that *the fame Perfon* both *fung* and *played* at the fame Time.

3. As thefe Paftorals are of two diftinct Forms, the one a *Monody* and the other a *Dialogue*; the Rules of Analogy lead us to believe, that the *paftoral Monody* was firft compofed and fung, becaufe it is the *fimpler Form*. It generally contains an artlefs Mixture of *Narration* and *Complaint*, the natural Effufions of Love and Grief.

4. The fame Rules of Analogy lead us to believe, that this *Monody* was naturally improved by Time, into the *paftoral Dialogue*. The *dramatic Form* was of Courfe introduced here, as it found it's Way into the grander Kinds of Poetry in GREECE.— I wonder, that none of the Critics have attempted to prove the *paftoral Dialogue*,

as well as the *tragic Dialogue*, to have been
a mere Imitation of HOMER. The *Odyſſy*
might have been as rich a Fund for the
one, as the *Iliad* for the *other*.—'Tis prefumed, it now fufficiently appears, that
the Poems of ESCHYLUS and THEOCRI-
TUS, no lefs than thofe of HOMER himfelf, were all of them *fair* and *blamelefs*
THEFTS FROM NATURE.

S E C T.   VIII.

*Of the Riſe and Progreſs of the leſſer Kinds
of Poetry in ancient* GREECE.

UNDER this Title of the *leſſer Kinds*
of Poetry, I include the *Elegy*, *Satire*, and *Didaɫtic*.

The *Elegy*, ſtrictly ſpeaking, is no other
than a Species of the *Ode :* It is properly
an *Ode* of *Lamentation.* The only Circumſtance, which in Proceſs of Time diftinguiſhed and identified This into a particular Species, ſeems to have been a peculiar Form of *Verſification.* There are
few remaining Models of This, among
the Greek Poets. EURIPIDES hath left
us *one* [k]. But this is a Progreſſion of
fuch a trifling Nature, as deſerves no
farther Notice.

[k] *Andromach.*

Satire,

Satire, in it's primary State, was likewife a Species of the *Ode.* As the *Elegy*
is an Ode of *Lamentation, Satire* was originally an Ode of *Invective.* In this Species of Compofition, we have feen, ARCH-
ILOCHUS was moft eminent [*l*]. It became afterwards a natural Appendage to
Comedy, when that Poem affumed it's legitimate Form. But I do not find that,
as a diftinct Species, it ever had any Progreffion in ancient GREECE.

With Refpect to the *Didactic ;* it appears above, to have had it's natural
Birth in the occafional Traits of *Remark,
Proverb,* or *Exhortation,* thrown out in
the Enthufiafm of the *mufical Conteft* or
Song-Feaft [*m*]. When Time, Experience,
and Letters, had ftrengthened the *reafoning Powers* of the improving Tribe, *then*
it would of Courfe receive the Addition
of *fpeculative* and *natural* Subjects. This
Improvement grew into a diftinct Species
in ancient GREECE ; but few of thefe
Poems have come down to us. Of this
Kind, it is manifeft from their Titles,
were many of the Songs of LINUS, OR-

[*l*] See above, Sect. vi. Art. 5.
[*m*] See above, Sect. iv. Art. 6.

PHEUS,

PHEUS, MUSÆUS, and THAMYRIS, compofed on the Generation of the World,
the Motions of the Stars, Chaos, Creation,
and the Rife of Things [n]. HESIOD's
Theogony ftill remains, as an original Model of this Species. Of the fame Kind is
his *Georgic;* which, though it be compofed on a Subject *œconomical,* is yet *effentially* mixed with Doctrines *religious, moral,*
and *political.* The *Sentences* of THEOG-
NIS are another Inftance of *this Species:*
which both with Refpect to it's legitimate
Form, and Dignity of Subject (ftill giving Allowance to the Manners and Opinions of the Times) feems to have received
it's full Completion in ancient GREECE.

S E C T. IX.

*On the Rife and Progreffions of Poetry,
in other European Countries.*

THUS we have traced the Progreffion
of the ancient *Greek* Poetry in all it's
Bránches, through the various Stages of
it's Power, down to it's final Corruption
in the later Periods. As a Confirmation
of the effential Principles offered in this
Difcourfe, let us now confider this natural

[n] See above, Sect. iv. Art. 9.

Pro-

Progreffion, as it hath appeared in other Nations, where the poetic Arts never arrived at fo compleat a Form ; where the Progreffion ceafed before any high Degree of Perfection came on, either through a Want of improving Literature, or by other Obftructions from internal or external Caufes.

The neareft Approach we can make to the favage State, in any Inftance drawn from the Records of Antiquity, feems to be found in the Hiftory of the *Cureles*, or *Corybantes* of the Ifland of CRETE. STRABO and DIODORUS, who give us their Hiftory, defcribe them as barbarous Tribes of Men, living among Caves and Mountains, at once *Warriors*, *Priefts*, *Poets*, and *Muficians ;* who celebrated their public Feftivals with enthufiaftic and clamorous Mufic, Song, and Dance, accompanied with Drums, Cymbals, and other noify Inftruments, almoft in the very Manner of the favage Iroquois [*o*]. RHADAMANTHUS firft, and then MINOS, civilized this barbarous Route ; and regulated their Manners and their Poem and Melody, on the Model of the fevere *Egyp-*

[*o*] STRABO, l. x. DIODORUS, l. v.

tion

tian Legiflation. After MINOS, THALES
arofe: In whom we find the united Characters of Legiflator and Bard: He compofed Laws, for the *Cretan* State, and
fung them to his Lyre [*p*]. But the poetic and mufical Arts being fixed to certain Forms by Law, we are not to wonder that their Progreffion ftopped, as at
SPARTA; which Commonwealth was
modelled on the rigorous Eftablifhment
of CRETE.

With Refpect to EGYPT, the Beginnings of that famous Kingdom are fo
loft in it's Antiquity, that we know nothing of the firft Advances there made
in Poem or Melody from their original
Savage State. We only read, that in fome
early Period of Civilization their Forms
were unalterably fixed by Law, and therefore all *Improvement* and *Corruption* alike
prevented.

As to the more *northern* Nations of *Europe,* it is remarkable, that we know little
of them from ancient Hiftory till the fecond

[*p*] As THALES fucceeded RHADAMANTHUS and
MINOS, who had *both* copied the EGYPTIAN Forms
of Legiflation; his compofing *Laws* in *Verfe* could only
be the Effect of mere *Imitation.*

N 4   Period

Period of Poetry and Mufic commenced,
that is, till the *Legiflator's* Character had
been *feparated* from that of the *Bard.*
The cleareft Inftance of the Union of the
Legiflator's and *Bard's* Character is found
in Snorro Sturloson, who, about five
hundred and fifty Years ago, was at once
the chief *Legiflator* and moft eminent *Bard*
in the Ifle of Iceland [*q*]. In the fecond Period, we meet with the poetic and
mufical Character united in almoft every
northern Clime, under the revered Deno-
mination of *Scaldi* or *Bards.*   It hath
been already obferved, that Odin the
Scythian Legiflator, boafted that the *Runic*
Songs had been given him by the Gods
[*r*]. A Circumftance which proves, that
the Character of *Heroe* and *Bard* had been
united in the Chiefs of that fierce and
favage People, in the Period which immediately preceded him. We learn from
Sheringham and Bartholine, that
after the firft Separation had been made,
that the *Scaldi*, *Muficians*, or *Bards*, were a
Race of Men highly honoured among
the *Scythian* or *Danifh* Tribes: That their

[*q*] Preface to Nicholson's *Irifh Hift. Library.*
[*r*] See above, Sect. v.

Songs

Songs were of the *legiſlative* Caſt ; that
they ſung the great Actions of their Anceſtors, were themſelves renowned Warriors, and kindled the Valour of their
Armies by their Songs : That none were
admitted of the Order, but thoſe of the
moſt diſtinguiſhed Families [*s*]: That they
were above the Meanneſs of Flattery ;
and were revered, even in the Courts of
Kings [*t*].

We meet with the *Gauliſh Bards* under
the ſame Period of Separation : But their
Spirit ſeems to have been controuled by a
more *peaceable* Species of Legiſlation. For
STRABO tells us, that " throughout the
" whole Diſtrict of GAUL, there are three
" Kinds of Men, who are held in ſingu-
" lar Honour: The *Bards*, the *Vates*, and
" the *Druids :* The *Bards* are *Poets*, and
" *ſing* their Hymns : The *Vates* perform
" *Sacrifice*, and *contemplate* the Nature of
" Things : The *Druids*, beſides this, hold
" Diſcourſes on *Morals*. They are eſteem-
" ed the juſteſt of Men ; and therefore
" are intruſted with the Determination of

[*s*] SHERINGHAM *de Angl. Orig.* p. 173.
[*t*] BARTHOLINUS *de Contemptu Mortis apud Danos,*
l. i. c. 8, 10.

" all

" all Differences, public and private ; and
" fometimes peaceably end a Quarrel,
" when Armies are drawn out, and ready
" to decide it by the Sword [*u*]." The
Evidence of DIODORUS is ftill more particular ; and proves, that they were not
infenfible to the original Sallies of comic
and farcaftic Wit. " They fing (faith He)
" to Inftruments refembling our Lyres ;
" *praifing* fome, and *fatyrizing* others.
" When Armies are ready to engage, if
" they but come between, they immedi-
" ately put an End to the Battle ; as if
" their Warriors were fo many wild
" Beafts, which they had charmed by
" the Power of their Songs [*w*].

The *Britifh Bards*, about the fame
Time, were precifely of the fame Charac-
ter ; as we learn from their contemporary
Roman Authors [*x*].   In a fucceeding Pe-

[*u*] L. iv.   [*w*] DIOD. l. v.

[*x*] A fingular Circumftance relative to the *Britifh*
Bards deferves Notice.   It is faid, that " although they
" were *inferior* to the *Druids* in *Rank*, yet they were
" *prior* in *Antiquity*." [SAMMES's *Phœnic. Ant. of Brit.*]
A Circumftance, which, though improbable in it's firft
Appearance, is clearly accounted for, on the Principles
of this Differtation ; as it only implies that *Melody* and
Poem were *prior* to *religious Rites*. [See Sect. iv. Art. 7.]

O   riod,

riod, when the Diftractions of our Country, had driven the native *Britons* into WALES, an *Englifh* King ftill felt their Power, amidft the Mountains and Poverty of that barren Region. He was fo highly exafperated by the Influence of their Songs, which breathed the Spirit of Liberty and War, and retarded his Conqueft over a hardy People, that he bafely ordered them to be flain: An Event which hath lately given Birth to an elegant and fublime Strain of Poetry [*y*].

Of

[*y*] An Ode, by Mr. GRAY.

The following Memoir, relative to the State of the *Welfh Bards* in fucceeding Times, may be acceptable to the curious Reader.

" By the QUEEN.

" ELIZABETH, by the Grace of GOD, of England,
"   France, and Ireland, Queen, Defender of the
" Faith, &c : To our trufty and right well beloved Sir
" Richard Bulkely Knight, Sir Rees Griffith Kt. Ellis
" Price Efq. Dr. in civil Law, and one of our Council in
" the Marcheffe of Wales, William Moftyn, Jeuen Lloyd
". Yale, John Salifbury of Rhug, Rice Thomas, Maurice
" Wynne, William Lewis, Pierce Moftyn, Owen John
" ap Howel Fichan, John William ap John, John Lewis
" Owen, Morris Griffith, Symnd Thelwat, John Grif-
" fith, Ellis ap William Lloyd, Robert Pulcfton, Harri
" ap Harri, William Glynn, and Rees Hughes Efqs.
" and to every of them Greeting."

" Whereas

Of the Genius of thofe *Britiſh Bards*
who inhabited the northen Diſtricts of the
Iſland, we have a noble Proof in the Poems
lately publiſhed under the Name of Os-
O 2   SIAN.

" Whereas it is come to the Knowledg of the Lord
" Prefident, and other our Council in our Marcheſſe of
" Wales, that vagrant and idle Perſons naming them-
" felves *Minſtrels, Rythmers,* and *Bards,* are lately grown
" into fuch *intolerable Multitude* within the Principality of
" North Wales, that not only Gentlemen and others by
" their *ſhameleſs Diſorders* are oftentimes difquieted in
" their Habitations, but alfo the *expert Minſtrels* and
" *Muſicians* in *Tonge* and *Cunynge* thereby much difcou-
" raged to travaile in the Exercife and Practife of their
" Knowledg, and alfo not a little hindred *(of)* Livings
" and Preferment ; The Reformation whereof, and the
" putting thefe People in Order, the faid Lord Prefident
" and Council have thought very neceſſary : And know-
" ing you to be Men of both Wifdom and upright Deal-
" ing, and alfo of Experience and good Knowledge in the
" Scyence, have appointed and authorized You to be
" Commiſſioners for that Purpofe : And forafmuch as
" our faid Council, of late travailling in fome Part of
" the faid Principality, had perfect Underſtanding by
" credible Report, that the accuſtomed Place for the
" Execution of the like Commiſſion hath been heretofore
" at Cayroes in our County of Flynt, and that William
" Moftyn Efq. and his Anceſtors have had the Gift and
" beſtowing of the *Sylver Harp* appertaining to the *Chief*
" of *that Faculty,* and that a *Year's Warning* (at leaſt)
" hath been accuſtomed to be given of the *Aſſembly*
" and Execution of the like Commiſſion ; Our faid
" Council

SIAN. Thefe appear to have been compof-
ed and fung, during the fecond Period of
Poetry and Mufic; that is, when the Bard's
Profeffion had feparated from that of the
Legif-

" Council have therefore appointed the Execution of
" this Commiffion to be at the faid Town of Cayroes,
" the Monday next after the Feaft of the Bleffed Trinity
" which fhall be in the Year of our Lord 1568. And
" therefore we require and command You by the Au-
" thority of thefe Prefents, not only to caufe *open Pro-*
" *clamation* to be made in all *Fairs, Market-Towns,* and
" other *Places of Affembly* within our Counties of Aglere,
" Carnarvon, Meryonydd, Denbigh and Flynt, that all
" and every Perfon and Perfons that intend to *maintain*
" their *Living* by Name or Colour of *Minftrels, Ryth-*
" *mers,* or *Bards,* within the Talaith of Aberffraw, com-
" prehending the faid five Shires, fhall be and appear
" before You the faid Day and Place to *fhew* their *Learn-*
" *ings* accordingly : But alfo, that You, twenty, nine-
" teen, eighteen, feventeen, fixteen, fifteen, fourteen,
" thirteen, twelve, eleven, ten, nine, eight, feven, or
" fix of you, whereof You the faid Sir Richard Bulkely,
" Sir Rees Griffith, Ellis Price, and William Moftyn
" Efqs. or three or two of you, to be of the Number ;
" to repair to the faid Place the Days aforefaid, and call-
" ing to you fuch *expert Men* in the faid *Faculty* of the
" *Welfh Mufick* as to You fhall be thought convenient, to
" proceed to the Execution of the Premifes, and to ad-
" mit fuch and fo many, as by your Wifdoms and
" Knowledges you fhall find *worthy,* into and under the
" *Degrees* heretofore *(in Ufe)* in femblable Sort to *ufe,*
" *exercife,* and *follow* the *Sciences* and *Faculties* of their
" *Pro-*

Legiflator, yet ftill retained it's Power and
Dignity in full Union. For Ossian, the
declared Author of the Poems, was the
Son of the royal Fingal, accompanied
O 3   him

" *Profeffions*, in fuch decent Order as fhall appertain to
" each of their Degrees, and as your Difcretions and
" Wifdoms fhall prefcribe unto them : Giving ftreight
" Monition and Commandment in our Name and on our
" Behalf to the reft not worthy, that they return to fome
" honeft Labour, and due Exercife, fuch as they be moft
" apt unto for Maintenance of their Living, upon Pain
" to be taken as fturdy and idle Vagabonds, and to be
" ufed according to the Laws and Statutes provided in
" that Behalf ; letting You with our faid Council look
" for Advertifement, by Certificate at your Hands, of
" your Doings in the Execution of the faid Premifes ;
" forefeeing in any wife, that upon the faid Affembly the
" Peace and good Order be obferved and kept accord-
" ingly ; afcertaining you that the faid William Moftyn
" hath promifed to fee Furniture and Things neceffary
" provided for that Affembly, at the Place aforefaid.

> " Given under our Signet at our City of Chefter, the
> " twenty third of October in the ninth Year of
> " our Reign, 1567."
>
> " Signed
> " Her Highnefs's Counfail
> " in the Marcheffe of Wales.

" *N. B.* This Commiffion was copy'd exactly from
" the Original now at Moftyn, A. D. 1693 :
" Where the *Silver Harp* alfo is."

From this Commiffion it appears, 1*ft*, That although
many of the *Bards* were maffacred by Edward the Firft,
yet

him in his Wars, and fung his Atchievements to the Harp. .Thefe Poems give
a noble Confirmation to many of the Principles advanced in this Analyfis. They
are of various Forms ; though none of
them properly unmixed. The *Song*, in
the Days of this fublime and original
Bard, appears evidently to have worn
the *inartificial* and *mixed* Forms of Compofition, which we have found generally
and of Courfe to prevail in the early Periods. Thus, FINGAL is chiefly *Epic* ;
yet the *hymnal* Species abounds in it:
Others are *dramatic* ; yet in thefe, the
narrative often takes Place : Others, again,
are in the Form of *Odes* ; yet even thefe

yet the whole *Order* was by no Means exterminated.
2*dly*, That in the Reign of ELIZABETH, Abufes had
crept on among the *Welfh Bards*, fimilar to thofe which
are recorded of the *Irifh*. 3*dly*, That public *Contefts* for
poetic and *mufical Fame* had been eftablifhed in *Wales* from
ancient Times. 4*tily*, That thefe Contefts are now
ceafed.

In Wotton's " Leges Wallicæ," (Append. p. 547,
548.) there are two Laws of Henry the Fourth recorded,
which relate to the Prevention of the Abufes of the Bard's
Profeffion ; but in fuch general Terms, that nothing relative to the particular State of their Mufic and Poetry
can be collected from them.

arc

are ftrongly mixed and marked with the
Epic and *dramatic* Manner [z].

The natural Flame of favage Mufic and
Poetry, is now almoft entirely quenched

[z] As thefe Circumftances are internal Proofs of the
Antiquity of the Poems ; fo there are other collateral
Evidences of the fame Nature, which feem clearly to
confirm it.   Such are the grand Simplicity of Imagery
and Diction, the ftrong Draughts of rude Manners and
uncultivated Scenes of Nature, which abound in all thefe
Poems ; Pictures, which no civilized Modern could ever
imbibe in their Strength, nor confequently could ever
throw out.   Such, again, are the frequent Allufions
(wrought into the very Effence of the Poems) to the Principles of the old *Celtic* Religion, which in ancient Times
had overfpread thefe Kingdoms : Of this Nature is That
which the Tranflator calls the *moft extravagant Fiction*
in all OSSIAN's Poems ; I mean, the Battle between
FINGAL, and the Ghoft or Spirit of LODA* : Now this
though it carries the Appearance of Extravagance and ill-
judged Improbability, yet, upon a nearer View, will be
found to contain an internal Evidence of the *Antiquity* of
the Poem ; as it is drawn from the very Effence of the old
Celtic Belief.   Thus fpeaks the learned BARTHOLINE :
—" Summa Audacia credebatur Lucta cum Spectris non
formidata †." " It was efteemed the higheft Act of Cou-
" rage, to dare to encounter a Ghoft."—But it muft be
obferved, that the Spirit of their chief God ODIN was an
Exception to this Rule : The Living and the Dead were
all deemed Subject to his Controul : therefore, the Spirit of LODA was not the Spirit of ODIN, but of fome
inferior Deity.

* *Carric-Thura :* A Poem.

† *De Contemptu Mortis apud Danos,* l. ii. c. 2.

in

in the feveral Parts of this Ifland. In *England*, it loft it's Power by the Migration of the native *Britons* into Wales: In Wales, it was fubdued by the Cruelty of Edward: In the Highlands of Scotland, the Writer is well informed, that the Bard's Profeffion was upheld in fome Degree of Honour, till near the Beginning of this Century. About that Time, the Communication of the Inhabitants with the more civilized Parts of the Kingdom by Degrees affimilated their Manners to thofe of their Neighbours; by which Means the Profeffion became extinct [a].

The Hiftory of the *Irifh Bards* is perhaps of all others the moft extraordinary; and will therefore deferve a particular Regard. Hiftory doth not carry us up to the firft Period, in which the *Legiflator's* and *Bard's* Character are united in the fame Perfon. But of the fecond

---

[a] About the Clofe of the laft Century, John Glass and John Macdonald, *Bards* by Profeffion, who refided and were refpected as fuch in the Houfes of two *Highland Chiefs*, travelled fifty Miles and met by Appointment in Lochaber, to vindicate their own Honour and that of their refpective Chiefs at a public Meeting, in a *poetic* and *mufical Conteft*.

Period

Period we have large Accounts in the
Irifh Hiftorians.   For we are informed,
there were three principal Tribes among
the ancient *Irifh*.   " The Firft were *Lea-*
" *ders, Chiefs,* or *Legiflators :* The Second
" were *Druids* or *Priefts :* The Third were
" *Bards*.   The two laft were honoured
" with an Appellation equivalent to the
" Name of *Gods* [b]."

The *Bards* had Eftates fettled on them,
that they might be free from worldly
Cares : They lived in perfect Independence, and were obliged to no Service:
Their Perfons were inviolable : To kill
them, was efteemed the blackeft Crime;
and it was held an Act of Sacrilege to
feize their Eftates, even for the public
Service, and in Times of the greateft Diftrefs [c].

The Profeffion was hereditary : But
when the *Bard* died, his Eftate defcended not to his eldeft Son, but to the moft
accomplifhed of his Family in the poetic
and mufical Profeffion.   A Law was made
by OLLAMH FODHLA, one of their
greateft Kings, that none fhould be in-

[b] KEATING's *Hiff.* of IRELAND, p. 48.
[c] Ibid. p. 132.

vefted

vefted with the Dignity of a *Bard*, but thofe of the moft illuftrious Families [*d*].

The *Bards*, the *Druids*, and *Nobility*, were fummoned by the fame King, to a *triennial Feftival*, which was thus by him eftablifhed, to tranfmit to Pofterity the *Authentic Songs* of the *Bards*, as the Materials of their future Hiftories. In Confequence of this, the approved Songs of the ancient Bards were preferved in the Cuftody of the King's Antiquary ; and are appealed to by KEATING, as the Foundation of his Hiftory [*e*]. Many of them were fabulous ; but this Circumftance hath no effential Relation to our prefent Inquiry [*f*].

Garments of different Colour were appropriated to the various Ranks of the Kingdom : So high was the Power and

[*d*] KEATING's *Hift.* of IRELAND, p. 132, &c.

[*e*] Ibid. p. 132. & Preface, p. 23.

[*f*] The Irifh Hiftorians inform us, that ST PATRICK, when he converted the Kingdom to Chriftianity, deftroyed no lefs than three hundred Volumes ,of thefe ancient Pagan Songs, on a Principle of religious Zeal. —How many FINGALS may *there* have been loft !—I fancy, a *Conclave* of *true Catholic Poets*, inftead of *fainting* him, would have fent him to *Purgatory* for his . Pains.

Dignity

Dignity of the *Bards*, that they wore the *fame Colour* with the *royal Family* [g].

Thus invested with Honours, Wealth, and Power; and poſſeſſed of an Art which gave them a natural Influence over the Minds of the People; we find, that about the Year 558, they had become inſolent, deeply corrupted, and dangerous.

Hence, the reigning King convened a general Council of the Nobility and Gentry (for Chriſtianity being now planted in IRELAND, the *Druids* were no more) with Intention to expel them the Iſland. They were now become a Kind of *ſacred Order*, or *College*; which was grown ſo numerous, that one third of the Kingdom is ſaid to have ranked themſelves in this Claſs, as a ſafe Aſylum for Idleneſs and Hypocriſy. When the *Principal Bards* aſſembled in a Body to divert this impending Storm, they met, to the Number of a *Thouſand*. This may account for the Numbers that claimed to be of the Profeſſion; for every *Principal Bard* retained *thirty* of inferior Note, as his Attendants; and a *Bard* of the *ſecond* Order

[g] KEATING'S *Hiſt.* of IRELAND, p. 127.

was

was followed by a Retinue of *fifteen.* In this Convention, after many Debates, it was refolved that they fhould leave the Ifland, and retire into SCOTLAND, before the Sentence of their Banifhment was pronounced.—However, the Sentence was mitigated: They were allowed to difperfe themfelves over the Ifland, and promifed to live in a Manner lefs offenfive to the Public [*h*].

In a fucceeding, and no very diftant Period, we find them again grown troublefome to the Kings, who complained of them, as a Burthen to the People, lazy, covetous, and infatiable. On this, their Number was leffened and regulated: By the Advice of St COLUM CILL., every provincial *Chief* had *one* learned *Bard* allowed him in his Retinue, to *record* the *Atchievements* of his Family: Their Independence, with a competent Revenue, was preferved: And this Regulation was the Standard, by which the Society of Bards were directed in fucceeding Ages [*i*].

'Tis to be obferved, that in fome unrecorded Period, a *Separation* had taken Place

[*h*] KEATING's *Hift.* of IRELAND, p. 370, &c.
[*i*] Ibid. p. 380, 381.

in the *Bard's* Profeſſion : In the early
Times, the Offices of *Poet* and *Lyriſt* were
united in the ſame Perſon : In the later
Ages, it appears, that the *Bard* only compoſed the *Poem* ; and that it was *ſung* by
a *Rhapſodiſt* or *Harper* at the public Feſtivals.

However, we find that on the Extinc-
tion of Learning, and Increaſe of Barba-
riſm in this Kingdom, the native Vigour
of the poetic Stock again ſhot up in a
ſucceeding Age ; and for Want of a proper
Culture, was again become one of the
ruling Evils of the Country, in the Time
of SPENSER ; Who gives the following
animated Deſcription of their *Songs* and
Character: " There is amongſt the *Iriſh* a
" certain Kind of People called *Bardes,*
" which are to them inſtead of *Poets,*
" whoſe Profeſſion is to ſet forth the
" *Praiſes* or *Diſpraiſes* of Men in their
" Poems or Rythmes ; the which are
" had in ſo high Regard and Eſtimation
" amongſt them, that none dare diſpleaſe
" them for Fear to run into Reproach
" through their Offence, and to be made
" infamous in the Mouths of all Men.
" For their Verſes are taken up with a ge-
" neral

" neral Applaufe, and ufually *fung* at all
" *Feafts* and *Meetings* by certain *other Per-*
" *fons,* whofe proper Function that is, who
" alfo receive for the fame great Rewards
" and Reputation amongft them."——
" Thefe *Irifh Bardes* are for the moft
" Part fo far from inftructing young Men
" in *moral* Difcipline, that they themfelves
" do more deferve to be fharply difcipli-
" ned: For they feldom ufe to choofe unto
" themfelves the Doings of *good* Men for
" the Arguments of their, Poems; but
" whomfoever they find to be moft *licen-*
" *tious* of Life, moft *bold* and *lawlefs* in his
" Doings, moft *dangerous* and *defperate* in
" all Parts of Difobedience and rebellious
" Difpofition; Him they *fet up* and *glorify*
" in their *Rythmes,* Him they *praife* to the
" *People,* and to *young* Men make an *Ex-*
" *ample* to follow."—Thus " evil Things
" being decked and attired with the gay
" Attire of goodly Words, may eafily de-
" ceive and carry away the Affection of a
" young Mind that is not well ftayed, but
" defirous by fome bold Adventures to
" make Proof of himfelf. For being (as
" they all be) brought up idely without
" Awe of Parents, without Precepts of
                                    " Mafters,

" Mafters, and without Fear of Offence;
" not being directed, nor employed in any
" Courfe of Life which may carry them to
" Virtue; will eafily be drawn to follow
" fuch as any fhall fet before them : For
" a young Mind cannot reft : If he be not
" ftill bufied in fome Goodnefs, he will
" find himfelf fuch Bufinefs, as fhall foon
" bufy all about him.   In which, if he
" fhall find any to praife him, and to give
" him Encouragement, as thofe *Bardes*
" and *Rythmers* do for little Reward, or a
" a Share of a *ftoln Cow*, then waxeth
" he moft infolent and half mad with the
" Love of himfelf, and his own lewd
" Deeds.   And as for Words to fet off
" fuch Lewdnefs, it is not hard for them
" to give a goodly and painted Shew
" thereunto, borrowed even from the Praifes
" which are proper to Virtue itfelf : As of
" a moft notorious *Thief* and wicked *Out-*
" *law*, which had lived all his Life-Time
" of *Spoils* and *Robberies*, one of their
" *Bardes* in his Praife will fay, that he
" was none of the idle *Milk-Sops* that was
" brought up by the *Fire-fide ;* but that
" moft of his Days he fpent in *Arms* and
" valiant *Enterprifes* : That he did never
                                  " eat

" eat his Meat, before he had won it
" with his Sword : That he lay not all
" Night flugging in a Cabin under his
" Mantle ; but ufed commonly to keep
" others waking to defend their Lives ; and
" did light his Candle at the Flames of their
" Houfes, to lead him in the Darknefs :
" That the Day was his Night, and the
" Night his Day : That he loved not to be
" long wooing of Wenches to yield to him ;
" but where he came, he took by Force
" the Spoil of other Men's Love, and
" left but Lamentation to their Lovers :
" That his Mufic was not the Harp, nor
" Lays of Love, but the Cries of People,
" and the clafhing of Armour : And fi-
" nally, that he died, not bewailed of
" many, but made many wail when he
" died, that dearly bought his Death."—
" I have caufed divers of thefe Poems to
" be tranflated unto me, that I might
" underftand them : And furely, they fa-
" voured of *fweet Wit* and *good Inven-*
" *tion ;* but *fkilled not* of the *goodly Orna-*
" *ments* of Poetry : Yet were they fprin-
" kled with fome *pretty Flowers* of their
" *natural Device,* which gave good Grace
" and Comelinefs unto them : The which
                                        " it

" it is *great Pity* to fee fo *abufed*, to the
" *gracing* of *Wickednefs* and *Vice*; which
" with *good Ufage* would ferve to *adorn*
" *and beautify Virtue* [*k*]."

This Account of the *Irifh Bards* is not
inferted here, as a mere Hiftory of Facts;
but with a farther View of confirming
the Principles on which this Differtation
is built. And the Writer thinks that all
the Facts (from the *early State* of the
Bards when they were efteemed as *Gods*,
down to their *laft Condition* when they
were funk into the *Abetters* of *Thieving*
and *Robbery*) arife fo naturally from the
Principles given above, that he is difpofed
to leave the particular Application to the
Reader's Sagacity.

S E C T. X.

Of the natural Progreffions of Poetry in
CHINA, PERU, *and* INDIA.

SUCH have been the natural *Progreffions* of *Poetry*, in the barbarous Nations of EUROPE. If we travel to the
Extremes of the Eaft and Weft, on the

[*k*] SPENSER's View of the State of IRELAND.

P   vaft

vaſt Continents of ASIA and AMERICA, we ſhall find new and ſtrong Confirmations of the *Progreſſions* of this Art, as it hath been here deduced from ſavage Life and Manners.

The *Chineſe* have ever been of a *mild* and *peaceable* Character: Their *Poem* and *Melody* will be found analogous. 'Tis generally ſuppoſed that CONFUCIUS eſtabliſhed their *Muſic* and *Rites:* but it appears from ſome curious Fragments of ancient *Chineſe* Hiſtory, that *Muſic* and the *Rites* exiſted in *Union* long before the Age of that Philoſopher [*l*]. TCHOYONG, the ſixteenth
" Emperor of the ninth Period, hearing
" a Concert of Birds, invented a Species
" of Muſic, whoſe Harmony was irreſiſt-
" able.   It touched the intelligent Soul,
" and calmed the Heart of Man ; ſo that
" the external Senſes were ſound, the Hu-
" mours in a juſt Poiſe, and the Life of
" Man lengthened [*m*]."   Here we find the genuine Picture of a *Chief*, at once *Legiſlator* and *Bard*, civilizing a ſavage People.

[*l*] *Extraits des Hiſt. Chinois*, publiſhed by Mr GoCUET, p. 550.   [*m*] Ib. p. 552.

The *Dance* was improved in the fame Manner, by the twentieth King of the ninth Period, to the Ends of peaceful Life [*n*]. And of fuch Importance has this Branch of the mufical Art been always held in CHINA, that it is an eftablifhed Maxim, " that you may judge " of any King's Reign, by the *Dances* " that are then in Ufe [*o*]."

.Thefe Evidences are traditionary, and relate to the fabulous Times : But even in a later Period, we find the *King's* and *Bard's* Character *united*, in the Perfon of FOU-HI, their firft great imperial Legiflator. " FOU-HI delivered the Laws of " Mufic : After he had invented the Art " of *Fifhing*, he compofed a *Song* for thofe " who exercifed that Art. He made a " *Lyre*, with Strings of *Silk*, to banifh all " *Impurity* of Heart : And in his Time " the *Rites* and *Mufic* were in great *Per-* "*fection* [*p*]." All this is evidently in the true Spirit of a peaceable Legiflation. " CHIN-NONG (a fucceeding Emperor) " compofed Songs on the *Fertility* of

[*n*] *Extraits des Hift. Chinois,* publifhed by Mr. CO-GUET, p. 555. [*o*] Ib. p. 556. [*p*] Ib. p. 567.

" the

" the Earth. He made a beautiful *Lyre*,
" and a *Guitar* adorned with precious
" Stones, which produced a noble Har-
" mony, curbed the Paffions, and ele-
" vated Man to *Virtue* and heavenly
" *Truth* [q]." This is the fame Character continued under a Period of higher
Civilization. The laft Emperor whom I
find to have retained the poetic or mufical Character, was Chao-Hao; who is
faid to have invented " a new Species of
" Mufic, to unite Men with fuperior Be-
" ings." After him, the *complex* Office
feems to have *feparated* : And the firft
great *Bardlike* Character we meet with
is Confucius, who eftablifhed *Mufic* and
the *Rites*, according to that Form which
they ftill maintain in China [r]. For
here, as in ancient Egypt, Crete, and
Sparta, every thing is unalterably fixed
by Law; by which Means, Improvement
and Corruption are alike prevented.

With Refpect to the Extent of the *Progreffion* of Mufic in this vaft Empire; it
appears that they have no mufical No-

<hr>

[q] *Extraits des Hift. Chinois*, publifhed by Mr. Goguet, p. 572.   [r] Du Halde *Hift. Chinois*.

tation;

tation; that Compofition in *Parts* is altogether unknown; and that the whole *Choir* fings the *fame* Melody: That their Mufic is altogether of the *diatonic Kind*, and even wretched to an *European* Ear [*s*]: Yet they boaft of it's wonderful Powers in former Times: Whence fome of the Hiftorians feem to guefs that it hath degenerated; while in reality, no other Confequence can be juftly drawn, but that either the People are lefs *ignorant* and *barbarous*; or that Mufic is now lefs affiduoufly and powerfully *applied*; or that certain *Separations* have enfued, fimilar to thofe which took Place in ancient GREECE: Any of which Caufes muft naturally deftroy it's Force.

It appears, however, that the Progreffion had advanced fo far in fome former Period, prior to CONFUCIUS, as to produce *dramatic Reprefentation*, mixed with *Song*: And in Conformity to the Principles given above, we find, that as they regard not the *Unities* of Action, Place, or Time, fo neither is any *continued Choir* in ufe; though there be manifeft Remains of it

[*s*] See Specimens of it, in DU HALDE.

in their *Plays*: For at the Conclufion of
Scenes or Acts, as well as at other Times
when a *pathetic* Circumftance occurs, the
Perfons of the Play, inftead of *declaiming*,
begin to *fing*. The *Prologue* refembles
that uncouth one of GREECE, that is,
he tells you *who* he is, and *what* is his
Errand. All their Plays have a *moral* or
political Direction, fuited to the Genius of
the People and the State. They know
not the Difference between *Tragedy* and
Comedy; another Circumftance which confirms the Principle given above, concerning the. true Rife and Diftinction of thefe
two Kinds in GREECE: For the *Chinefe*,
as they have ever been of a *timid* and
peaceable Character, fo neither are they
given to *Raillery* or *Sarcafm*, but altogether
to *Civility* and mutual *Refpect*. Hence,
neither the *tragic* nor *comic* Drama could
probably arife, fo as to be marked as a
diftinct Species. Accordingly, their *Plays*
are generally of an *intermediate* Caft, between *Terror* and *Pity* on the one Hand,
Sarcafm or *Ridicule* on the other. The
" *little Orphan* of CHINA," indeed, which
is given as a Specimen by DU HALDE,
borders on the *tragic* Species: But this

Play

Play is but one of a hundred, moft of
which are of a different Caft; and was
felected by him, becaufe he thought it the
beft adapted in it's Genius, to the Spirit
and Tafte of the *Europeans :* For he tells
us exprefly, that the general Character of
their Plays is altogether different from
this; that they are commonly of a *middle* Kind, and neither *Tragedy* nor *Comedy.* Another Circumftance of the Progreffion muft be marked; which is, that
their *Actors* are a *feparate* Rank from their
Poets; that they are formed into *Companies,* and have loft their original Dignity of Office and Character.

In the ancient Kingdom of PERU,
the Progreffion of *Poem* and *Melody* had
reached the fame Period, though fomewhat different in it's Circumftances. GAR-
CILASSO DE LA VEGA informs us, that
their fabulous Songs were innumerable;
that he had heard many, and learnt fome of
them, from his Anceftors, who were the laft
of the royal Family of the INCAS. They
were of various Kinds, founded on a Variety of Paffion, religious, warlike, and
amorous. They had invented a Kind of
unequal Pipe, formed of Reeds of different
P 4   Lengths,

·Lengths, precifely the fame with that of ancient GREECE. They had alfo a Species of Flute, with four or five Stops: Their Mufic was fimple, like that of all unpolifhed Countries. Their INCAS or *Chiefs* had been *Poets* or *Bards* in the early Periods; and the Author of the Commentaries gives a Poem compofed by one of them, which bears all the Marks of a fpirited and favage Original. They had their *dramatic* Reprefentations, in Part *refembling*, and in Part *differing* from thofe of the *Chinefe*. Their Manners and Character, *brave* though not *ferocious*, had naturally produced *Tragedy*, though of a Kind rather *grand* than *terrible* [*t*]. But their *mild Temper*, in Time of *Peace* little given to *Sarçafin*, feems to have *prevented* the Birth of *Comedy*. GARCILASSO, indeed, divides their *Drama* into *Tragedy* and *Comedy*: But this was manifeftly the Effect of his own preconceived Opinions, and arofe from a Habit of confidering all *dramatic* Compofition as belonging to one of thefe *Species*. For he tells us that " their *Tragedies* reprefented their military " Exploits ; the *Triumphs*, *Victories*, and

[*t*] See above, Sect. v. Art. 22.

heroic

" *heroic Actions* of their renowned Men :
" And the Subject or Defign of their
" Comedies was to demonſtrate the Man-
" ner of good *Husbandry* in *cultivating*
" and manuring their *Fields*, and to ſhew
" the Management of domeſtic Affairs, with
" other familiar Matters." A Circumſtance,
which ought to give them the Title of
Bucolic or *Georgic Drama*, rather than that
of *Comedy*. For not a Word occurs concerning *Ridicule* or *Character ;* the *Union*
of which two Circumſtances may feem
to conſtitute the *Eſſence* of *true Comedy.*
Theſe Plays were *compoſed* by the *Amau-*
tas or *Bards*, whoſe Office was ſeparated
from that of the INCAS, but ſtill held
in Honour, as in other barbarous Polities.   But in another Reſpect, the Progreſſion was different from that in CHI-
NA.   The *Actors* maintained the original
Dignity which they had held in the early
Periods : For the *Lords* and *Officers* of
the Court were the *Actors ;* and as foon
as the Play was ended, they took their
Places according to their *Degrees* [*u*].

[*u*] GARCILASSO DE LA VEGA *Comment. Real.* l. ii.
c. 14. 15.

To

To thefe we may add one Inftance more, concerning the natural Progreffion of Poetry : An Inftance lefs known, yet more fingular than any of thefe already given. When the *Chriftian Miffionaries* arrived on the Coaft of *proper India*, they found a Sect called the " *Chriftians of St.* THO- " MAS," living in great Simplicity and Innocence ; and retaining many of the original Cuftoms of their favage Forefathers [w] ; among others, they found thefe Chriftians, as well as the Pagans of the Country, poffeffed of rude *Poetry* and *Mufic*, in their *natural Union* and *Power*. They acquiefced in the Application of thefe Arts, already made by the Chriftian Tribe, and wifely laid hold of their Influence, for the Converfion of the Pagan Natives. Under thefe Circumftances, the following Accounts will appear natural and probable, on the Principles already delivered.

Firft, it appears, that the general and fundamental Practice of *finging* the *Praife* of *great Men*, had been maintained from the moft ancient Times. In Confequence

[w] LA CROZE *Hift. du Chrift.* p. 38, &c.

of

of this, " The Synode being ended, the
" Partifans of the Union compofed in the
" *Malabar* Tongue a long *Ode* or *Song*,
" which contained the whole *Hiſtory* of
" the *Portugueſe Prelate*, and a pompous
" Detail of what had paſſed at the Sy-
" nod. This Nation hath preferved the
" ancient Cuſtom of confecrating to Poſ-
" terity by this Kind of Poem all the
" moſt remarkable Events.   The Song
" was caught and immediately difperfed
" every where ; and during the Vifits
" which the Prelate made, the People
" fung it in his Prefence ; which to-
" gether with their *Dances* and *Muſic*
" made the chief Part of his Entertain-
" ment [*x*].   When he went to Anga-
" male, the Way was fpread with Car-
" pets : And it was a fine Sight, to fee
" a *Child* of fix Years old, very beauti-
" ful, and richly dreſſed, who *fung* melo-
" dioufly the whole *Song* we have fpoken
" of, as containing the *Labours* of the
" *Prelate* [*y*].

The religious *Song* and *Dance* were no
lefs remarkably and fingularly maintained

[*x*] La Croze *Hiſt. du Chriſt.* p. 282.
[*y*] Ib. p. 294.

in

in a Kind of imperfect *Union,* as they
had been transferred from *Pagan* Objects to thofe of *Chriftianity.* " In the
" fame Place, the *Chriftian Malabars,* to
" amufe the Archbifhop, gave him a *Ball*
" after the Manner of the Country. It
" was of fo fingular a Nature, that I am
" perfuaded, the Reader will not be dif
" pleafed with the Defcription. Thefe
" *Dances* are generally practifed at *Night.*
" This begun at Eight in the Evening,
" and lafted till an Hour after Midnight.
" None but the Men dance ; and their
" Modefty and Referve are admirable.
" Before the *Dance* begins they all make
" the *Sign* of the *Crofs,* and *fing* the *Lord's*
" *Prayer,* which is followed by a *Hymn,*
" in Honour of *St. Thomas.* Their other
" *Songs* rowl chiefly on the *illuftrious Ac-*
" *tions* of their *Forefathers,* or the *Virtues*
" of their *Saints.* In a Word, this Enter-
" tainment has all the Air of *an Act of*
" *Devotion ;* on which the *Portuguefe Hif-*
" *torian* takes Occafion to inveigh againft
" the *prophane Songs* of the *Europeans,*
" which feem compofed only to infpire
" *Debauch* and *Immodefty* [z]."

[z] L.A CROZE *Hift. du Chrift.* p. 296.

The

The Miffionaries who have vifited the
oppofite Coaft of CoROMANDEL, give us
Proof, that the *Progreffion* of *Poetry* had
not ftopped at this early Period, but advanced to *threatrical Reprefentation;* which,
we fhall fee, they were bold enough to
apply even to the great Purpofe of *Converfion.* " In this Country they have an
" extreme Paffion for the *Theatre.* Good
" Poets are held in great *Veneration* among
" this People, who are by no Means of
" a barbarous Caft.   In INDIA, Poetry
" enjoys the Favour of the Great. They
" give it's young Profeffors the Honour
" of the *Palanquin,* which is a very
" high Diftinction.   The *Theatre,* which
" was prepared near our Church, was of
" vaft Extent.   Indeed I found not there
" the Rules of HORACE or BOILEAU put
" in Practice ; but was agreeably fur-
" prized to find the *Acts* diftinguifhed,
" and varied with *Interludes* or *Choirs,*
" the Scenes well connected, the Ma-
" chines judioufly invented, Art in the
" Conduct of the Piece, Tafte in the Dref-
" fes, Propriety in the *Dances,* and a Kind of
" *Mufic,* harmonious though *irregular* and
" *wild.* The *Actors* difplayed great *Free-*
dom

" *dom* and *Dignity* in their Speech: They
" were taken from one of the *Superior*
" *Orders* or *Caftes*.   Their Memory was
" good, and there were *no Prompters.*
" That which edified me moft was, that
" the Piece began with an authentic
" Profeffion of Chriftianity : And con-
" tained the keeneft *Ridicule* and fevereft
" *Invectives* on the *Gods* of the Country.
" Such are the *Chriftian Tragedies*, which
" they oppofe here to the *prophane Tra-*
" *gedies* of the *Idolaters* [*a*] *;* and they are
" for this Reafon, an excellent Mean of
" Converfion [*b*].—The Audience was com-
" pofed of at leaft twenty thoufand Souls,
" who liftened in profound Silence.—The
" Character of their Theatre is that of a
" *lively* and *perpetual Action ;* and a ftrict
" Caution of *avoiding long Speeches,* with-
" out proper *Breaks* [*c*].

Such is the State of *Poem* and *Melody*
in proper INDIA.   Some of it's Appear-

[*a*] Hence it appears that the *Hiftory* of their *Gods*
made the Subject of their *native* theatrical Reprefentations.

[*b*] How far this was a proper Method of Converfion, will be confidered in the Work advertifed at the .
End of this Differtation.

[*c*] *Lettres Edifiantes, Recueil,* xviii. p. 28.

ances

ances are fingular ; and at firft View, may feem unnatural. But after a mature Confideration of what has been delivered on the Rife, Union, Progreffion, and Separation of thefe Arts in ancient GREECE, 'tis prefumed, the fenfible Reader will eafily account for all thefe apparent Singularities.

S E C T. XI.

Of the State of Poetry amongft the ancient Hebrews.

LET us now, in Conclufion, analyze the State of *Poetry*, among the ancient *Hebrews*.

The leading fingularity of this extraordinary People was their Rejection of Idolatry, and their eftablifhed Worfhip of the *one* GOD, the *Creator* of the World. As this Circumftance gave a peculiar Colour to their *Religion ;* fo, upon the Principles of this Differtation it will follow, that it muft give a Peculiar Turn to their *Poetry*, becaufe we have feen, that the Genius of the *original Poetry* of every Country depends on it's *Religion* as it's chief *Bafis.*

In

In Confequence of this Principle, their Poem was chiefly dedicated to the *Celebration* of the *true* God, the *Creator* of all Things : At other Times it is compofed of *moral Exhortations*, delivered as the Dictates of his Will, or thrown out in prophetic Raptures concerning the great Intents of his Providence.—Hence the *Hymn, Ode*, or poetic *Rapture*, which we have found to be naturally the firft Form of Compofition among all Nations, appeared with unrivaled Splendor in the *Hebrew* Poetry, becaufe it's *Object* is fo much *Superior* to that of other Nations : The one being no more than the limited and narrow Power of fuppofed *local Gods ;* the other, the Omnipotence and Wifdom of an *eternal* and *univerfal Creator.* Of this Diftinction their *Bards* were fully fenfible. " As for the Gods of the Hea- " then, they are but *Idols ;* but it is the " *Lord*, that *made* the *Heavens."* The Book of Pfalms, the Lamentations, the Songs of Moses, David, Isaiah, and other Prophets, all written in Meafure, and fung by thofe who compofed them, are fo many ftriking Inftances of the true and unequaled Sublime.

With

With Refpect to the *Form*, it may be obferved, that their *Songs* or *Hymns* are of that *mixed* Species which naturally arifeth firft, before any Separations take Place, or produce the feveral diftinct Species of Compofition. Though the *hymnal* Form be chiefly *predominant*, yet we find them frequently to be a Mixture of *Ode*, *Narration*, and *Dialogue*; and thus they contain the Seeds or Principles of the three great fucceeding Kinds, of *unmixed Ode*, *Epic*, and *Tragedy*.

It may be regarded as an extraordinary Circumftance, that this firft *mixed* Form of Compofition fhould have continued unchanged for a Period of at leaft a thoufand Years; and that from firft to laft it fhould never move forward, fo as to produce the *Epic* and *Dramatic* Species: But on Examination it will appear, that the fame Caufe (the Worfhip of the one GOD) which produced the higheft Degree of Sublime in the *hymnal* Species, naturally *checked* the Courfe of Poetry among the JEWS; and prevented that *Progreffion* which we have found to arife from the natural State of Things, in *Pagan* Countries.

With Refpect to the *Epic* Poem, we have feen that, in it's firft and original Conception and Formation, it is no other than " A fabulous Hiftory, rowling chiefly on " the great Actions of the Gods and He- " roes of the Nation; and compofed un- " der certain Limitations with Refpect to " it's Manner, for the Ends of Pleafure, " Admiration, and Inftruction." Hence, the *true* GOD being the fole Object of the Adoration of the HEBREWS, and their Records being the facred Depofitary of the *Hiftory* of his *Providence*, the Truth of which it was deemed the higheft Crime to violate; the Invention and Conftruction of an *Epic Fable* could never be the Refult of a *natural* and *untaught Progreffion*.

If the *Epic* Form was thus naturally prevented by the Severity of Truth, the firft Form of *Tragedy*, and *dramatic Exhibition* muft of Courfe be checked from the fame Principle: For we have feen that the native and original *tragic* Species is but an *Union* of the *Ode* and *Epic* Fable animated by *perfonal* Reprefentation. To this we may fubjoin, that an additional Abfurdity would here prefent itfelf: The Abfurdity of cloathing the *Deity* in a vifible,

ble and *human Form :* A Circumſtance ſtrictly forbidden by the *Jewiſh* Law.

If it be ſaid, that although theſe Reaſons are good, againſt their introducing the *Deity* as the leading Subject either of *Epic* or *dramatic Fable,* yet ſtill their *Heroes* might have furniſhed Subjects for *Both :* We may reply, that all the great Actions of their Heroes were ſo intimately connected with the important Hiſtory of Providence, which this People were deſtined both to *execute* and *preſerve,* that even *Theſe* became improper Subjects for the Mixture and Alloy of Fable. And farther ; The very Tendency of Fancy towards ſuch a Progreſſion of Poetry was quenched *here* alſo, in it's firſt Conception. For the firſt and original Enthuſiaſms of an untaught Tribe are awakened by the Belief, that their deceaſed Heroes are advanced to the Rank of *Gods,* and ſtill maintain their former *Relation* and *Affection* to their native *Country :* Hence the Imagination is kindled by Hope of their Favour and Aſſiſtance : Hence Adoration riſeth ; flattering Fables of their Power, Prowefs, and Atchievements are invented ; and the Genius of *Epic* and *Tragic* Song is awakened into Action.   But where (as among the JEWS) their greatest Men are reprefented as what they were, weak, ig- . norant, and mortal; often humbled for their Sins; always under the Controul of an over-ruling Providence; and after Death, loft to every earthly Connection; here, the firft natural Enthufiafms of the Soul could meet with no Objects to excite them: A Collifion was wanting: And the artlefs Mind, inftructed only in facred Things, returned of itfelf to the unmixed and inartificial Celebration of the *all-wife* and *all-powerful* GOD.

As, from thefe Caufes, the Forms of their *Poem* never had any Progreffion; fo, it feems probable, that their *Melody* ftood ftill, in the fame Manner.   It's Applica-tion was chiefly to the Service of Religion; and as their Hymn continued unchanged in it's Genius, we may reafonably believe that the Melody which accompanied it, had the fame Fate.   For though there was nothing particular ordained, with Refpect to Mufic, in the *Mofaic* Law; yet, where almoft every other Circumftance relative to Worfhip was particularly prefcribed, this Severity of Inftitution would give a

Kind

Kind of Sanctity to every ancient Custom that stood connected with it; and hence their Modes of Melody would probably remain unchanged.   CLEMENS ALEXAN-DRINUS informs us, that their Hymns were compofed in the *Dorian* Mode [*d*]: Which, whatever it was, we know to have been one of the moft *ancient*, as well as *grave* and *fedate*; and therefore fit for the Service of the Temple.—Their Inftru-ments were various, but fimple: That which DAVID chiefly ufed, appears to have been the *Nabla* or *Trigonon*; a three-cornered Inftrument, of the *Harp*-Species. It's Compafs we know from his own Au-thority; and that it was an Inftrument of *ten Strings*.   We may be affured, too, that his Melody was not only fimple, but fingle: For he muft have held his Harp with one Hand, and played with the other, when he led the *religious Dance* before the Ark.

As their *Poem* and *Melody*, fo their *Dance* feems to have been chiefly em-ployed in the Service of Religion.   The moft frequent Exercife of this religious

[*d*] STROMAT. l. vi.

Q 3   Rite

Rite devolved upon the Women. It appears too, that the Prophets had some
Kind of *solemn Movements*, suited to the
State and Circumstances of their divine
Enthusiasm: This Branch of the *triple
musical Alliance* seems (as in other Countries) to have made the earliest Separation.
It appears to have been chiefly exercised
by the lower Ranks, in the Time of DA-
VID: And hence it was, that MICHAL,
the Daughter of SAUL, like a true fine
Lady, despised that Monarch, for exerci-
sing a Mode of Piety, which in her Days
was *no longer fashionable*.

As to the united or complex Character
of *Legislator* or *Bard*, it is remarkable,
that this was preserved among the JEWS
through a longer Succession of Ages than
in any other Nation, from the same Cause
which prevented any Progression or Change
in the Forms of their Song: For the musical Art being chiefly exercised in the
Praises of the true GOD, was in less Danger of being *corrupted*, and therefore not
only it's *Utility* was longer *preserved*, but
likewise it's *Professors* were in less Danger
of being *debased*, than in other Countries
where trifling or immoral Applications of
the

the Art enfued.   Confequently, the Rulers
of the People could have no Temptation
to quit any Part of that Character or Office, which ftill maintained it's priftine
Ufe and Dignity.   Accordingly, we find,
that from MOSES down to SOLOMON,
during a Period of at leaft a thoufand
Years, the *complex* Character of *Legiflator*
and *Bard* often appeared in the moft diftinguifhed Leaders of their State, and
from firft to laft remained unbroken.
MOSES, their firft great Lawgiver, led the
Song of Triumph, on the Overthrow of
the *Egyptians* in the *Red-Sea* [*e*]: MI-
RIAM, a diftinguifhed Prophetefs, led the
female Dance and Choir, on the fame Occafion [*f*].   While the *Judges* ruled in
ISRAEL, this complex Office ftill remained: DEBORAH is an Inftance of this
Truth: She *judged* ISRAEL; and fung
her noble Song of Triumph, on the Death
of SISERA and JABIN.   We find, that
whoever was raifed to the Station of a
Judge, or *Chief,* was commonly invefted
not only with the *prophetic* but the *bard-
like* Character: For we know, that the

[*e*] EXODUS.   [*f*] Ibid.

Prophets generally fung their prophetic Raptures to the Harp [g]. In After-times, when SAUL was elected *King*, he too aſſumed at once the prophetic and muſical Office. The Songs and bard-like Powers[1] of DAVID, his *kingly* Succeſſor, are two well known to need an Illuſtration. The fame muſical and poetic Character maintained it's Union with that of *King*, in his Son SOLOMON; whofe *Songs*, we are told, were no leſs than a *thouſand and five*. After him the *complex* Office of *Legiſlator* and *Bard* feems to have *feparated* : The peculiar Caufes which had fo long upheld it in the *Jewiſh* State, now began to ceafe : For *Idolatry* more and more prevailed, *Manners* became *corrupt*, and public Mifery and Ruin enfued. The *Prophets* and *Bards* were now no longer found in the Courts of Kings, or among the Rulers of the People : Yet ſtill they continued to throw out the Emanations of prophetic and moral Truth, accompanied with the Enthuſiafm of *Song*, in the more retired, and yet uncorrupt Situations of private Life : And fuch were the

[g] 1 SAM. X.—1 CHRON. XXV.

Later

later Prophets, whose Writings still remain in Scripture.

As this appears to be a true Analysis of the State of *Poetry* among the ancient HEBREWS ; it will now lead us to an easy Solution of a Fact which hath been regarded as mysterious by some of the Learned ; " That while most other " Nations had their *Bards* or *Poets ;* the " JEWS, though their Compositions are " uncommonly sublime, never had any " *Poets by Profession,* nor even a Word " in their Language which denotes the " Character [*b*]." The Principles here given afford a clear Solution of this Singularity. Their *Prophets* were indeed their *Bards ;* and appear to have been invested with all the Dignity belonging to that Office in it's most honoured State. But as the Almighty GOD, and the great Events of his *Providence,* were the continued *Object* of their *Songs ;* so, the *poetic* or *musical* Character was but *secondary* to the *religious ;* Therefore the Name of *Bard* was swallowed up and lost in the higher Title of " *The* PROPHET *of the* " MOST HIGH."

[*b*] CALMET. *Differt. sur la Poesie,* &c.

SECT.

S E C T. XII.

Of the State of Poetry in ancient ROME.

WE have now traced the Progress of
Poetry, through the most remarkable Periods of those various Nations, in
which it's *Rise* and *Progress* was *native*
and *original.* Let us now view it in it's
more *weak*, and *borrowed* State.

The first Flight which *Poetry* took from
GREECE was to ROME: For in this imperial City it was not *native.* The Causes of this original Defect, together with
the State and Progressions of this Art at
ROME, on it's Arrival from GREECE, will
make the Subject of this Section.

The only Cause that hath been af-
signed for the Want of Poetry among
the *Romans* in the early Ages of the Republic, hath been " that their Attention
" to War and Conquest swallowed up all
" other Regards ; and therefore Poem and
" Melody were of Course neglected." This
Reasoning might hold, if these Arts made
no more than a mere *Amusement* in the
early Ages, as they generally do in the
later

later Periods of a State.   But as it appears in the Courfe of this Diffcrtation, that they are the *natural* Produce of *favage* Life, however *warlike*; that the Continuance of this *warlike* Character tends rather to *heighten* than *extinguiſh* their Power; and that the Hiſtory of human Nature confirms this Truth; We muſt therefore feek for this peculiar Defect in fome other, and more hidden Caufe.

There is a Principle which relates to the Eſtabliſhment and *Character* of *Colonies*, which will hereafter appear attended with extenfive Confequences, and which will aſſiſt us in unfolding the true Foundation of this Defect.

Poem, Melody, and *Dance,* being the natural Effects of favage Manners continuing through feveral Ages, it muſt follow, that *Colonies* will in general be found to poſſefs them in a very imperfect State; if we regard them as being of *Influence* on the *Manners* of a People. For *Colonies* are feldom fent out, till that early Period is paſt, when the *Legiſlator's* and *Bard's* Character are *united* in the fame Perfon. Hence the *Leader* of the new Colony not being poſſeſſed of the poetic and mufical

Enthu-

Enthufiafm, can neither have *Ability* nor *Inclination* to inftil or propagate thefe Arts
among his Followers, as the Means of a
farther Civilization. Thus the firft *leading Flame* of *Enthufiafm* is *quenched :* And
the inferior Ranks, being bufied in the
Affairs of their new Settlement, have not
that Leifure which the unemployed favage
State affords, to turn their Attention on
thefe natural Pleafures : For Colonies of
Men feldom depart from their native
Country, unlefs when driven by fome
Kind of *Neceffity :* And therefore muft
betake themfelves, for Subfiftence, either
to *Induftry* or *War.* The laft of thefe
was the chief Occupation of the *Roman*
State : And thus, not becaufe they were
a *warlike* People, but becaufe they were
a *needy Colony,* the *mufical Arts* which
were fo *powerful* in *early* GREECE, were
fo *weak* in *early* ROME.

This Obfervation will hold true of moft
other Countries peopled by foreign Nations *after* a *certain Period* of *Civilization.*
Thus CARTHAGE was a Colony which
went out from TYRE : And *Poetry* and
Mufic, which were of Weight in the *native*
City, were of no Confideration in the *de-
fcendant*

fcendant State.   Thus again, the *Irifh*, *Welfh*, and *Scots*, are ftrictly *natives ;* and accordingly have a Poetry and Mufic of *their own :* The *Englifh*, on the contrary, are a foreign Mixture of *late-eftablifhed* Colonies ; and as a Confequence of this, have *no native Poetry* or *Mufic*.   He who would find the *original Poetry* and *Mufic* of ENGLAND, muft feek it in WALES.

Here, then, appears the true Caufe of this Defect in the early Ages of ROME. So ignorant were the *Trojan* Founders of the Empire in the poetic and mufical Arts, that they had not even the firft Rudiments of *Song :* For we are told by a learned *Roman*, that when ENEAS brought the Images of the Gods to Shore, " the *Women howled* and *danced* at the " Solemnity [i]."

The Hiftory of the poetic and mufi- cal Arts in ROME confirms this general Principle : Their Poetry and Mufic was always *borrowed* and *adopted :* Let us trace it's Progrefs through the feveral fucceed- ing Ages.

NUMA POMPILIUS firft introduced thefe Arts into the *Roman* religious Ceremonies.

[i] DIONYS. *Halicarn,* l. i. c. 55.

Had

Had he been a *Native* of ROME, he had
been a clear Exception to the Principle
here given : But inftead of overturning,
he confirms it : For he was a retired, philofophic, and illuftrious *Sabine* : And the
Salian Priefts which he eftablifhed, were
Muficians or *Bards*, who had been brought
by EVANDER from ARCADIA into ITALY
[*k*]. Thus, the *Salian* Songs were not
native, but *tranfplanted* into ROME.—The
Authority of QUINTILIAN confirms this
Account. " Thefe *Salian* Songs (faith
" he) were inftituted by NUMA ; and
" prove, that *Mufic* was not difregarded,
" even in that *rude* and *warlike* Age [*l*].

We find no farther Progrefs in the
poetic and mufical Arts, for many Ages:
Save only, that a vague Rumour prevailed
in the later Periods of the Commonwealth,
that in ancient Times it had been ufual
to fing the Praifes of great Men at
Feafts [*m*].

The next Progreffion of thefe Arts in
ROME, was the *Adoption* of the *Thufcan
Shews :* Thefe, as LIVY informs us, were
called in from ETRURIA during a fatal

[*k*] DIONYS. *Hal.* l. i.   [*l*] L. i. c. 17.
[*m*] CICERO *de Leg.* l. ii.

Peftilence, with a View of appeafing the angry Gods [*n*].   The borrowed Flame was foon caught and fpread among the *Roman* Youth ; who by Degrees gave *Voice* to the *mute Action* of the *Thufcans.*

To thefe the *Atellane* Plays fucceeded; being in the fame Manner *borrowed* and adopted by the *Roman* People from the Osci, a neighbouring Province : Both thefe, and the *Thufcan Shews,* feems to have been *native* in their refpective Dif-ftricts ; and therefore we need go no far-ther in Queft of their true Origin, than to the untaught Progreffion and Separa-tion of *Melody, Dance,* and *poetic Song :* But on their firft Entrance into ROME, thefe dramatic Shews were no longer in their *natural,* but in an *ingrafted* State.   The firft Idea, then, of *Comedy,* was caught by *Adoption* in this Republic : Here, as in the Adoption of the *Salian Songs,* they were mere *Imitators.*   And thus, contrary to the natural Courfe of Things (as we have proved above [*o*]) *Comedy* had, by Accident, an Eftablifhment prior to *Tra-gedy* in ancient ROME.

[*n*] LIV. *Hift.* l. vii.   [*o*] Sect. vii.

As

As it appears that in the firſt Periods
of theatrical and dramatic Repreſentation,
it is natural for the *Poet* to *act* a Part
in his own Plays [*p*] ; ſo Livius An-
dronicus, the firſt known dramatic Poet
of Rome [*q*], maintained this natural
Union of the *Poet* and *Actor*, which he
had received from the *adopted Shews.*
But ſo little were theatrical Repreſentations the Effect of Nature at Rome, and
ſo much were they received as mere
Shews of *Pleaſure* and *Amuſement*, that
even at this early Period an unexampled
Separation commenced; a Separation more
abſurd than any that had taken Place
in Greece. For now, " Livius acting
" his own Play according to the Cuſtom
" of the Times, was compelled by the
" People to repeat ſome favourite Paſſa-
" ges, till his Voice grew hoarſe : On
" which, he obtained Leave to ſubſtitute
" a Slave to *ſing* the Poem along with
" the *Muſician*, while he himſelf performed
" the *Action* in dumb Shew [*r*]." Thus
an *abſurd Separation* was eſtabliſhed ; and
continued ſo eſtabliſhed through the ſuc-

[*p*] Sect. vi.   [*q*] Art. 26.   [*r*] Liv. *Hiſt.* l. vii.

ceeding

ceeding Ages of the *Roman* Empire [*s*]. Hence ROSCIUS himſelf, of whom the World hath heard ſo much, was often no more than an Imitator by *mute* Action. We may ſafely pronounce it impoſſible that this Separation could have come on, unleſs the theatric Repreſentations had already degenerated into a mere *Amuſement*. When a *Slave* was permitted to *ſing* the *Poem*, we may be ſure the chief Attention was turned on the *Geſticulation* of the *Actor*.   That which in a *ſound* State of Things had been *ſubordinate*, was now become *principal*.

However, the theatrical Shews in this Period ſeem to have had little Effect; the Manners of the People continuing much the ſame with thoſe of more ancient Times.   After the Succeſſion of a few Ages, the principal Progreſſions came on; and theſe aroſe from their Acquaintance with, and their Conqueſt of GREECE.

As this Event happened many Years after the poetic and muſical Arts had loſt their *Union*, their proper *Ends*, and original *Genius* in the *Mother-Country*; ſo it

[*s*] LUCIAN *de Salt.*

R   was

was natural, that the *Romans* (now verg-
ing towards a Decline of Manners) fhould
greedily borrow and adopt them, in that
feparate, imperfect, and *perverted* State
which thefe Arts held when the *Greeks*
were conquered by the *Romans.* Let us
therefore trace them from their firft to
their laft Progreffions in ROME; where
we fhall find, that from being of mere
Amufement or little Utility, they degenerated by Degrees into Things pernicious.

In the early Periods of GREECE, the
Poet compofed the Melody for his Plays:
In the Decline of the Greek States, the
Melody was the diftinct Labour of another Perfon [*t*]. This Separation the
Romans maintained : A Conduct natural
among thofe who confidered thefe Arts as
the Inftruments of Pleafure only. The
neceffary Confequence of this was the gradual Introduction of an effeminate and
luxuriant Melody; of which both CI-
CERO [*u*] and Horace [*w*] in their refpective Times complain.

In Confequence of thefe, a new and
fatal Separation enfued. The *Player,*

[*t*] See above, Sect. vi. Art. 35.
[*u*] *De Leg.* L. ii.   [*w*] *Epift. ad Pif.*

who

who in the uncorrupted Ages of GREECE was often of the *firſt Rank* in the Republic, was generally of *ſlaviſh* Birth at *Rome;* and was by Law excluded from the Freedom of the City [*x*].

A whimſical Change was made in the Form of the *Maſque* : For in order to give a *Variety* of *Expreſſion*, which became neceſſary as the Fable of their Comedy grew more *complicated*, the two Sides were marked with *different Paſſions.* " The " Father, who is a principal Character in " the Comedy, as he is ſometimes *pleaſed*, " and ſometimes *angry*, hath one of his " Eyebrows even, and the other *raiſed* " aloft: and the *Roman* Actors take Care " to ſhew *that Side* of the *Maſque* to the " Audience which ſuits with his *preſent* " *Temper* [*y*]."

Such were the Progreſſions in the *Exhibition* of their *Comedy.* With Regard to the *Compoſition*, PLAUTUS hath left us the cleareſt Proof, that in the early Periods they had adopted the coarſe Manner of the *old Greek Comedy :* And TERENCE remains an indiſputable Evidence, that in a later Age

[*x*] LIV. *Hiſt.* L xxiv.   [*y*] QUINTIL. *Inſt.* l. ii. c. 11.

they

they copied (though weakly) the Elegance and Graces of Menander.

As we have now feen, that *Comedy* had an *accidental* Eftablifhment prior to *Tragedy* (contrary to the natural Courfe of Things) from the mere Principle of *Imitation;* fo we find, that their *Tragedy* had it's Rife and Cultivation from the fame accidental Source, prior to the *Ode* and *Epic,* in a Way no lefs contrary to the *natural Progreffion* of thefe feveral Species : For we have feen above [z], that the Greek Tragedy was the native Offspring of the *conjoined Ode* and *Epic.* But with Refpect both to the *Subjects* and *Form* of their *Tragedy,* the *Romans* were *mere Imitators.* For although they had one Species in which their own Great Men were the *Heroes* of the Poem, yet even this was not original, but altogether built on the *Grecian Model.* But farther, we learn from Horace, that the moft approved Subjects were thofe which were drawn from Homer's Poems. He gives this as a Rule to the Poets of his Time and Country; "That to "throw the Fables of the *Iliad* into tragic "Scenes is a fafer and better Practice,

[z] Sect. iv. Art. 17.

"than

" than to attempt Subjects yet untouch-
" ed."   A Paſſage which contains the
cleareſt Proof, that Tragedy was now
ſeparated from it's higheſt Purpoſes ;
and that the *great Ends* of this *Poem,*
which gave it ſo much Power in GREECE,
were utterly loſt to the Roman People.

The primary Application of *Tragedy* being thus little known in ROME, even
on it's firſt Admiſſion ; we cannot wonder that it became a weak and languid
Amuſement : Eſpecially, among a People
whoſe Manners were now ſinking into
That Character which tended to give *Comedy* the Aſcendant, as in the declining
Period of the *Greek* States.   Thus again
the true Cauſe appears, why *Comedy* was
cultivated ſo much more than *Tragedy,*
in *every Period* of this Republic.

The *Ode* or *hymnal* Species ſeems to
have been equally the Effect of mere Imitation ; and no leſs generally ſeparated
from the Ends of *Public Utility*, than the
Tragic Poem.   HORACE often declares
his Inability to attempt any thing *Great*
in this Kind.   The general Character of
his Odes correſponds much with his own
Sentiment : They are always elegant, ſel-

dom majeſtic. His *Irreligion* even *diſqua-
liſied* him from excelling in the *higheſt Species* of the *Ode :* For of this, we have
ſeen, *Religion* muſt be the *Object :* And
although there be a Variety of fine *moral* Apothegms, and frequent Alluſions to
the *public State* of ROME; yet theſe are
always *checked*, and made *ſubſervient* to
the Favour of MÆCENAS and AUGUS-
TUS. In a Word, they are but *ſecon-
dary : Urbanity* of Sentiment, *Elegance* of
Phraſe, and of *Compliment* to his Maſters,
were manifeſtly his *firſt Object.*

With Regard to the Character of the
famed *Roman Epic* Poem ; notwithſtand-
ing the inordinate Praiſes that have been
laviſhed on VIRGIL's *Æneid*, it may
with Truth be affirmed, that neither the
original nor *legiſlative* Spirit of ancient
GREECE appear with any *uniform* Splendor through the Courſe of this celebrated
Work. Elegant in Diction, a Maſter in
Rythm and Numbers, nervous in Figures,
majeſtic in Deſcription, pathetic in tragic
Incidents, ſtrong in the Delineation of
Character, accompliſhed in all the *ſecon-
dary Qualities* of an *Epic Poet ;* yet ſtill
VIRGIL wanted that all-comprehenſive
Genius

Genius which alone can conceive and
ftrike out a great original Epic Plan, no
lefs than that independent Greatnefs of
Soul which was quenched by the *ruinous Policy* of the Times, and which alone
can animate true Genius to a full Exertion of it's Powers in the Caufe of *public Virtue* and *Mankind.* Through the firft
of thefe Defects, the *Æneid* abounds with
falfe Pictures of refined Manners, with
Incidents that are borrowed, unconnected,
broken, and ill-placed ; through the fecond, though here and there the Spirit
of *general Legiflation* appears [*a*], yet the
great Subjects *peculiarly relative* to the
Roman State, the *Glories* of the *Republic*,
the *Atchievements* of it's *Heroes*, all thefe
are caft into *Shades*, and feen as through
a *Veil ;* while the *ftrongeft Lights*, and
higheft Colourings of his Pencil are *profti-
tuted* to the *Vanity* of the *ruling Tyrant.*

LUCAN, in a later Period, feems to have
poffeffed the true Spirit of *Roman Legiflation*, in Spite of the terrible Caprices of
a remorfelefs Tyrant, and the Enormity
of the Times in which he lived. But
he came too late, to obtain a favourable

[*a*] See Div. Leg. of Mofes, B. i. Sect. 4.

R 4   Hearing

Hearing from his Countrymen. *Public Spirit* was now no more: fo that LUCAN's was an Attempt to *raife* the *Dead.* Befides this, the Period which he chofe for the Action of his Poem was fo *recent,* that *Truth* could not *bend* to *Fiction:* He appears, farther, to have been an *Orator,* rather than a *Poet.* Yet, amidft all thefe Defects, we muft acknowledge, that both in the *Choice* and *Profecution* of his *Subject,* he was more truly *Roman* and *Original* than the divine VIRGIL.

As to the *Paftoral Species;* in this, too, the *Romans* were mere Imitators. Many of VIRGIL's Scenes and Lines are no more than elegant Tranflations from THE-OCRITUS. As the mere Principle of Imitation, when incautioufly purfued, will always be fruitful of Abfurdities; fo VIR-GIL, while he copied the *external Forms* of the *Sicilian Bard,* loft the *internal Part,* the *native ruftic Manners.* And for Want of *drawing after Nature,* hath often made his *Shepherds* talk like *fine Gentlemen.*

Some of the leffer Kinds of Poetry, though all borrowed from GREECE, were imitated more confiftently. The *Elegy* was formed and fixed by a peculiar Species of

Ver-

Verfification: And it's Subject being chiefly that of *private Diſtreſs*, it eaſily retained it's original Nature, through all the various Revolutions of Times and Manners.

The *Didactic* was honoured by the Attention and Art of the two greateſt Poets of Rome. Lucretius hath given us Proof, that Philoſophy may be adorned by the ſublimeſt Strokes of Genius. And were I (like Scaliger) to build an *Altar* to the *divine* Virgil, it ſhould be for the Production of his immortal *Georgic;* which undoubtedly ſtands in the firſt Rank of human Compoſitions.

As it is evident that Homer was Virgil's Model in the *Epic*, Theocritus in the *Paſtoral*, and Hesiod in the *Didactic Species*, we may now diſcover the Reaſon, " why the ſame Poet who fell ſo " far ſhort of the *two former* in his Imi- " tations, ſhould ſo far have excelled the " *third*." In his *Epic*, he had the great Taſk to accompliſh, of painting thoſe *ancient Manners* which he had *never ſeen;* and in his *Paſtoral*, thoſe *ruſtic Manners* which he was *little acquainted with.* Thus the Foundations of his Art ſunk under his Genius; and in both Inſtances a falſe

Re-

Refinement in Manners became a ruling Defect. But in the Construction of his *Georgic*, he had no such Difficulties to cope with. *Unknown Manners* made no Part of his Subject : For his Subject was the *Tillage* of the *Earth :* Now, in the Words of an ancient Sage, " One Generation of " Men passeth away, and another cometh; " but *the Earth abideth for ever :*" And the general Rules of *Tillage* being easily learnt from *his own Observations* on the Practice of his Countrymen and Contemporaries, he became a *Master of his Subject :* He *painted* what he *saw :* he delivered his *Precepts* at once with *Dignity*, and according to *Nature :* Thus he produced a Poem, in every Respect worthy of his exalted Genius ; and while he kept his Model in his Eye, became himself a *true* and a *great Original.*

In one Respect, however, it is necessary here to remark HESIOD's *Superiority* over his two *great Imitators ;* I mean, in the superior Tendency of his Work considered in a *legislative* View, and it's salutary Influence on *Manners.* It hath been observed above [*b*], that though his

[*b*] Sect. viii

Subject

Subject be merely *œconomical,* yet " it is
" effentially mixed with Doctrines *religi-*
" *ous, political,* and *moral.*"   But the whole
Poem of LUCRETIUS is a bold Difplay
of an atheiftic Syftem :   And fome incidental Paffages in VIRGIL's *Georgic* are
manifeftly built on the fame *pernicious*
Principle.

Satire was not only happily imitated,
but improved into a *diftinct Species ;* and
exalted, from an *Ode* of *vague Invective,*
into a *moral Difcourfe,* marked with ftriking Characters ;   and tending to public
Utility, by the fevereft Sarcafms thrown
on Vice, and the moft generous Commen-
dations of Virtue.—It may feem an unaccountable Circumftance, that " when
" Manners were degenerating at ROME,
" and other Kinds of Poetry had loft
" their proper Ends, this *moral Species*
" fhould arife in it's *greateft Vigour.*"   But
the Solution to this Difficulty will naturally
emerge from a deeper View of the State
of Things at ROME.   For the *moral Satire*
requiring for it's full Exertion and Completion, not only a *refined* and *eftablifhed*
Diftinction between *moral Good* and *Evil;*
but likewife a general *Departure* from the
firft,

firſt, and *Proneneſs* to the *latter*; we ſee, that on theſe Foundations, *moral Satire* ſhould naturally appear in it's *Strength*, in a *late* and *declining Age* [*c*].

To return, therefore, to the decaying State of the poetic and muſical Arts in ancient R O M E.—As Manners and Principles grew more profligate, along with the inordinate growing Power and Luxuries of the Empire; ſo the Genius of the *poetic* and *muſical* Arts kept Pace with them. We hear little of their being applied to the *Education* of *Youth*, in any

[*c*] As moſt of the poetic Kinds (*Satire* excepted) had thus degenerated from their original Character in GREECE, ſo we ſhall find that the *Recitation* of them kept Pace with this ſpurious Birth. We have already ſeen, that in the more early Periods of the *Greek* Republics, their Poems were *ſung* to the ſurrounding Audience for the important Ends of *Religion*, *Morals*, and *Polity*. In ROME, as in the later Periods of GREECE, we find the *Song* brought down to *Recitation*, and theſe *great Purpoſes* ſwallowed up and loſt in the *Vanity* and *Self-Importance* of the *Poet*. Hence we find their beſt Writers declaring their Diſlike to the Practice of *public Recitation*, becauſe Flattery was now become the Food of every reciting Poetaſter. The whole Farce and Foppery of this Practice, which was indeed no other than the ſpurious Iſſue of the old *Grecian Song-Feaſt*, is given at large by Vossius, to whom, for Brevity's Sake, we refer *.

* *De Imitatione*, c. 7, &c.

Period

Period of ancient ROME. On the contrary ; *Poem*, which in the Days of ancient GREECE had been the *Handmaid* of *Virtue*, was now declared to be the *Bawd* of *Licentioufnefs* ; and to write *immodeft* Verfes was held a *blamelefs* Practice [d]. Thus the Art funk fo low, that the Name of *Poet* was held unworthy a Man of *Age* or *Dignity* [e]. The *mimetic* and *mufical* Arts grew not only an intolerable Burthen, but became at length of moft pernicious Influence on the State. The Attention to the *mimetic* Art was now carried to a moft ridiculous Extreme. CICERO informs us, that the Players practifed feveral Years, before they ventured upon the Stage [f] : That the Actors, in Imitation of the degenerate *Greeks*, gradually awakened their Powers of Speech in the Morning, left by too fudden an Exertion they fhould endanger the Voice [g]. They gargled the Throat with a Compofition proper. for the Purpofe : And the Methods of managing and improving the Voice were

[d] *Caftum decet effe Poetam : Ipfos Verficulos nihil neceffe eft.*   [e] *Turpe eft Senem Verfus fcribere.*
[f] CIC. *de Oratore*, l. i.   [g] Ibid.

now formed into a feparate Science [*h*].
In a Word, LIVY complains, that "an
" Amufement which was harmlefs in it's
" Beginnings, had now grown to fuch a
" Madnefs of Expence, that the wealthieft
" Kingdoms were hardly equal to it [*i*]."

In the later Periods the Mifchief grew
ftill more intolerable : For now, the ferious Arts were cultivated by Few : Nothing was heard but light and effeminate
Mufic : The Singer took the Philofopher's
Place ; the Libraries were fhut up ; and
the general Attention was turned upon
mufical Inftruments proper to accompany
and fuftain the Gefticulation of the Actors.   The Effects of this Diffolute Tafte
foon appeared : for QUINTILIAN tells us,
that " the effeminate and immodeft Mu-
" fic of the Stage had no inconfiderable
" Part in deftroying that fmall Degree of
" manly Character which had been left
" among them [*k*]."

The Evil ftill increafed : So that in the
Time of NERO, " The City fwarmed with
" *Pantomimes :* Every private Houfe now
" became a Theatre ; and the Hufband
" and Wife contended, which fhould moft

[*h*] PERSIUS *Sat.* I.   [*i*] L. vii.   [*k*] *Inft.* l. i.

" fuc-

" fuccefsfully *proftitute* themfelves to the
" *Favour* of the *Actors* [*l*]."

There is a Time, when Nature ftrug-
gles hard to free herfelf from peccant and
deadly Humours. This Time was now
come at Rome ; but it came too late:
The Body politic was expiring, and was
not able to fhake off the Evil: The Pantomimes were twice expelled ; but ftill
returned again [*m*]. At length, the barbarous Nations of the North broke in
upon the dying Empire. Totila attacked and pillaged Rome: The degenerate Arts funk with the degenerate City:
And the Patrician Ladies, who lately had
reveled amidft the Spoils of a fubjected
World, now begged before their own
Doors.

The extravagant Paffion of fome of their
late Emperors for the mufical Arts, and
thefe too of the moft debauched and profligate Characters, particularly Caligula
and Nero, is too well known to need a
Delineation: But on this Subject, there is
one Circumftance which may demand our
Regard. We have feen above, that the

[*l*] Seneca *Nat. Quaft.* l. vii.
[*m*] Tac. *An.* l. xiii, xiv.

firft

firft original Legiflators turned their Attention ftrongly on the mufical Arts ;
and we now find, that the abandoned
Rulers of a decaying Empire adopt them
with no lefs Eagernefs : Doth not this
Contrariety of Facts feem to fhake fome
of the Principles which we have attempted
to eftablifh ? So far from this, that it confirms them : For in both Inftances, *Poetry*
and *Mufic* were made *fubfervient* to the
Views or ruling *Paffions* of thofe who *led* the
People. The honeft Legiflators of early
Times employed them for the Ends of public Utility ; the profligate Emperors abufed them to the Purpofes of Licentioufnefs.
Among the former, by a legitimate Ufe,
they became the Inftrument of eftablifhing
Commonwealths : Among the latter, by a
perverted Application, they fhook the Foundations of Empire : ORPHEUS drew the
barbarous Tribes from Theft, Adultery,
and Murder, by his *Songs* and *Lyre* :
NERO plundered his Patricians of their
Eftates to load his *Players* and *Muficians*
with Wealth ; and while he exercifed and
excelled in the *refined Arts*, violated a *Vef-
tal*, and killed his *Mother*.

SECT.

SECT. XIII.

The Conclusion.

THUS the *poetic* and *musical* Arts sunk along with the *Roman* Empire. —But Mankind, emerging from the Ruins of *Luxury*, *Profligacy*, and *Invasion*, are of a different Character from that of human Nature arising from mere *Barbarity* into *Civilization.* We have traced the natural Progress of these Arts among the latter; but from the *former*, nothing consistent or steady can arise. The Views, Manners, Principles, and Passions of a furious Conqueror, meeting and mixing with those of a subdued and abandoned People, produce such a Compound of dissimilar and contending Causes, as approach in their Effects to the Appearance of mere Chance or Fortune.

But the Circumstance most worth remarking is this, that in such a Period, all the natural Seeds and Principles of the *poetic* and *musical* Arts are lost. The whole *local* Fabric of *Religion*, *Polity*, and *Morals*, is commonly sunk in the general Ruin; and a barbarous Conqueror followed by an enraged Soldiery, who have

S   left

left their own Country to invade another, have generally the *Vices* of *Savages*, without their *Virtues*.

Hence the *poetic* Arts could not arife from the Ruins of the *Roman* Empire, but from the ineffectual Principle of *mere Imitation*. They wanted that *native* Force and Vigour which had given them so free and full a Growth in ancient Greece.

Such therefore being the Birth of the *modern Poetry* of Europe ; having been the cafual Offspring of the corrupted *Roman* Arts, which were themfelves no more than partial Imitations of the *Greek*, in their State of Separation and Weaknefs ; no Wonder if the *modern Tranfcript* be *inferior*, not only to the *Original*, but the *firft Copy*.

Here then, for the prefent, the Writer clofeth his Analyfis. To purfue this Principle of Imitation through the fucceeding Periods, and point out the various Forms of Poetry which it hath produced in different Times and Countries, down to the prefent Age, may perhaps be the Subject of a future Inquiry.

T H E   E N D.

By the fame AUTHOR,

With all convenient Speed will be publifhed,

PRINCIPLES

OF

CHRISTIAN LEGISLATION,

IN EIGHT BOOKS.

BEING

An Analyfis of the various Religions, Manners, and Polities of Mankind, in their feveral Gradations:

OF

The Obftructions thence arifing to the general Progrefs and proper Effects of Chriftianity:

AND OF

The moft practicable Remedies to thefe Obftructions.

Things, from an Union of the *Narration* and the *Choir*, without any Refpect had to HOMER's Poems. The fame Arguments that have proved the one, will confirm the other. We fee the natural Seeds of Comedy and fcenic Reprefentation in favage Life, no lefs than thofe of Tragedy [*o*]: Nay, even in the earlieft Periods of GREECE itfelf, we fhall find the firft rude Form of Comedy, arifing from an Union of *dramatic Reprefentation* and a *Choir*, long before HOMER exifted. In the Account already cited from STRABO and others, of the *mufical Conteft* eftablifhed at DELPHI, which in Time branched out into the equeftrian and gymnaftic Games, as we have found the firft rude Form of *Tragedy;* fo now we fhall find likewife a faint Outline of the firft rude Form of *Comedy.* For it appears, that APOLLO with his Choir, and his Worfhippers, in after-times, not only reprefented his Victory, and fung a Pæan in Confequence of it (in which Union we fee the firft rude Form of Tragedy) but likewife, in the Way of Ridicule they reprefented the *Hif-fes* of the dying Serpent, and fung an *In-*

[*o*] See above, Sect. ii.

vective

" compleated the Form of the Epic Po-
" em [*n*]."   That Homer, as well as other
Bards of the early Periods, fung their comic Poems at the feftal Solemnities, needs
no farther Proof here.

   3. " From thefe two Species (the *Choral*
" and *Narrative* united) the firft rude
" Outline of Comedy arofe."   The *Narrative*, already animated by a lively Action,
did eafily flide into *dramatic* Reprefentation;
and the correfpondent Peals of *Laughter*
excited among the furrounding Audience,
by means of written Invectives, affumed
the Form of the *comic Choir*.   In this
Point, we have again to contend with the
general Body of Critics, from Aristotle
down to the prefent Times, who all con-
cur in afcribing the Rife of the legitimate
Form of Comedy to Homer's *Margites;*
in the fame Manner as they have afcribed
the Rife of *Tragedy* to the *Iliad* and *Odyffy.*
But notwithftanding this general Concur-
rence of Opinion, it feems evident that the
Progreffion of Comedy was founded in the
fame Caufes with that of Tragedy: That
they both naturally arofe in the Courfe of

[*n*] *Poët,* c. 4.

M 2   Things